An Integrated Life of Leadership: 20 Years of Nurturing & Inspiring Others to Reach for the Stars

All We Feared
By David Sirgany

After eons of countless thresholds
another edge appeared

On that luminous precipice
We surrendered all we feared

Now this mind was still and silent
as the spinning world just spinned

In those final moments
my heart
became
the wind

DEDICATION

We'd like to dedicate this book to all leaders, emerging and experienced. We hope you find joy and inspiration in the pages that follow. May you always follow your heart and your dreams come true.

Table of Contents

ACKNOWLEDGMENTS

Thank you to David Sirgany for allowing the use, for cover art, of his painting, "My Heart Became the Wind," which has been inspiring Ginny and her team for years.

Thank you to Kaitlea Toohey for cover formatting and design.

Thank you to everyone who shared their personal stories, insights, and advice.

FOREWORD
BY RANDY MOORE

I have worked in leadership roles for the last several decades. I have had the privilege of working with an array of individuals on different levels. Being a Black American, I think it is my duty to make sure I am giving back to my community. The best way I can do this is to make sure I am serving as best as possible in the leadership position I hold. Being an example of all that is good, but keeping it real, is the right thing to do. Operating with integrity and focus is one of the key elements missing from a lot of the leadership in this country today. Demonstrating a degree of wholeness is vital.

I graduated from Indiana Wesleyan with a Master's in Business Administration (MBA) in 1999. I was ready to face the business world and take it on without regard. However, while I was well versed in the logistical side of operating a business, I had to develop a skill set for leading a business. Most of those who I had worked with before were terrible leaders. Therefore, I did not have a deep pool of resources to dive into when it came to getting advice on leadership. I did as most people do; I had to lead by trial and error. Sometimes it worked and sometimes it didn't. One day while trying to navigate through a difficult operational situation, it occurred to me that the best way to lead was to treat people the way I wanted to be treated. It sounds like a simple concept, but in my career, not many people seemed to understand this concept. Leadership for me is a choice that is filled with so many different options.

In 2010, I moved to Davenport, Iowa, to take on the toughest leadership role in my career. I had managed to survive several mergers and downsizings in my company and was now assigned to sit in the most challenging seat I have ever sat in before. As the CEO and President of my subsidiary company, I was not only the top person, I was the most visible person for the company. I met Ginny at the retirement event for my predecessor. I knew that I would need support in not only managing this new role but great assistance in learning how to implement all that I had learned in my past experiences. I also knew that there was much more for me to learn and that I would need to connect with the right person to teach me those special nuances that you cannot pick up from a textbook as it relates to leadership. Ginny Wilson-Peters from Integrity Integrated was that person. Ginny has shown me how to flip the mirror around and to look at me first instead of trying to get others to see themselves. Once I was able to grasp a better understanding of me, it became easier to lead others. Ginny has helped me immensely through this understanding process.

The fact that Ginny is willing to share her expertise with others is a huge benefit to those she serves. Her students and clients are blessed to simply be in her presence. She radiates positivity and exudes personality. Her teaching, training, and coaching styles are exemplary and should be experienced by all who desire to be or are currently in a leadership role, regardless of the industry. Her company, Integrity Integrated, works to improve individuals' realizations of who they are, what they can do, and how to make it happen. The inner core of a person's leadership ability is exposed in her classes. Female, male, black, white, Latino, or whatever you are or want to be, she really takes who you are and shows you how to use "you" as an advantage in leadership.

This book will be a world changer. Ginny sharing her stories and real-life experiences in this book is a mammoth opportunity for those not fortunate enough to be geographically close to her, to experience some of her life-altering talents. Her personal passion and commitment to helping others achieve their personal and professional goals are both surprising and refreshing to all who read the book. Reading it will not only entertain you, but it will also educate you and prepare you for challenges you have yet to face.

I do not think this book is for any one particular group of people. I believe this book is for everyone. If you are not in a leadership role and had not really considered moving into leadership, this book is something to which you should give serious consideration. We all serve as leaders at some point in our lives. We take leadership roles as mothers, fathers, aunts, uncles, and grandparents. We take leadership roles in church groups, neighborhoods, schools, on the job, and the list goes on and on. If there is any desire to improve yourself for others, or improving others for the betterment of the day, this is the tool you should have in your Leadership Development Tool Box.

My tenure with Ginny over these several years has been inspiring. She is eloquent, professional, and is intellectually competent enough to be heard by all levels. The personal and professional experiences she has managed make her a very qualified candidate to produce an educational, professional, and palatable book such as this.

Happy reading.

FINDING CLARITY

THE VISION:
TODAY IS JULY 23, 2007

I am 46 years old. I love my life. Greg and I live in a three-bedroom house outside of the Quad Cities in Illinois with our three dogs. Our five acres include woods and a lake. This morning I saw a deer, several rabbits, and two raccoons before I left for work.

I am surrounded by nature. I am blessed with a husband who I dearly love, and who loves and supports me in all my craziness. We are planning a trip to Puerto Vallarta in November next year to celebrate our ten-year wedding anniversary.

My nieces and great nieces have just left after an annual two-week visit with us. I love having their young feminine energy around and will miss having them here.

My work aligns with my purpose in life to nurture and inspire others to reach for the stars.

Integrity Integrated offices are located in the Village of East Davenport. In addition, we have a building on our acreage that houses another office space for me as well as space for one-day and weekend retreats.

Professionally, I am a recognized expert in teaching

leadership. I am teaching three MBA classes and one Executive MBA class per year for the University of Iowa. I love teaching.

In addition to teaching, my focus is on groups (corporate, women, and Chamber leadership) and one-on-one coaching. I am working with people who are committed to creating sustainable change in their leadership behaviors through a clear vision and acting in alignment with their values and mission in life.

People participating in group sessions leave feeling nurtured by the supportive and challenging environment created by the group. Additionally, they leave motivated to create change in their lives.

One-on-one coaching clients leave their sessions with an experience of having been really heard—and respected for who they are. During the sessions, they gain clarity on their issues in a compassionate and direct way.

I am taking master's level courses in diversity and cultural competency. I am also actively involved in learning, practicing, and teaching Native American traditions.

People I work with stay connected to one another via online chat rooms hosted by Integrity Integrated.

Integrity Integrated has a staff of two full-time people who assist with research, website development, marketing, and clerical work.

JULY 2007

That was the vision. How does that compare with current reality? Two years ago, Greg and I found the house of our dreams and moved into the country. We now live on three acres of wooded land with four bedrooms and one dog. When we moved in, there was a creek on one side of our property but no lake. This past spring, a large pond developed in the lower level of our property. The pond stayed for almost two months and was home to many ducks and other wildlife while it was there. We hope to see it return again next spring.

We didn't wait for our ten-year anniversary; we returned to Puerto Vallarta for our six-year anniversary and plan to return to Mexico for our ten-year.

We do have a building on our property that will someday house office space and retreat space. That hasn't happened yet, but it is there.

My work is very close to that described in the vision. This past year, I taught three MBA classes, including an executive MBA class in Hong Kong. I am not enrolled in a master's level program for cultural competency, but I am studying and practicing Native American traditions.

Integrity Integrated has a staff of one person in addition to me, and she does assist with all of the items described. No, we don't have chat rooms yet but are investigating the possibility of using blogs to help people stay connected.

*****

This is the exact wording of Ginny's vision for her life five years out from 2002. At the time it was written, Ginny and her husband were living in town, and she was the only person working for Integrity Integrated. The subsequent entry also contains Ginny's exact words, written in 2007 as a reflection of how her vision materialized.

This was Ginny's vision. How did she make it happen?

To become truly happy in your life and step fully into the leader you were born to be, you must first become clear about your strengths, core values, passion, and life purpose. We can trace Ginny Wilson-Peters' life purpose, which is to nurture and inspire others to reach for the stars, to her childhood.

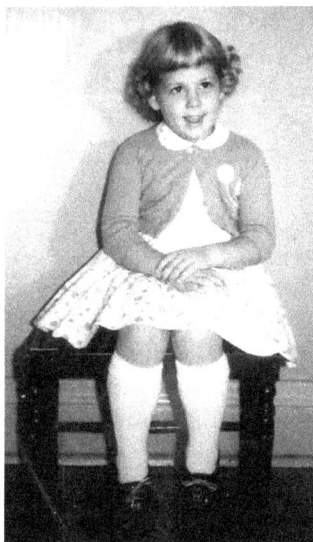

Ginny at five years old.

Ginny grew up in the country outside of Colo, Iowa, a small town of fewer than 1,000 people outside of Ames. Transportation prohibited many visits with friends, so she took advantage of having her three older brothers around as her playmates. She would've been considered a tomboy since she followed them everywhere and had to step out of her comfort zone to keep up with them. She also spent a lot of time alone reading at home.

Growing up, Ginny got involved in Girl Scouts and

stayed involved until she was in high school. Though she wouldn't consider herself a leader "in charge" of anything, she helped with a lot of events and always went away for a week or two in the summertime to camp. Ginny also found success in softball, receiving recognition for her skills as one of the best in the area in Iowa. These experiences taught Ginny that she could get recognition for working hard and doing a good job.

If you had to point to a precise moment that could foreshadow Ginny's purpose, one of them would be when she attended her brother's high school graduation. During one of the commencement speeches, she knew then and there that she wanted to be a public speaker. And she told herself she would do that someday.

Ginny was the first and only person in her immediate family to go to college. She chose the University of Iowa because Iowa State, in Ames, was too close to home. She studied finance and started her first career at RSM McGladrey as an auditor before moving up to manager and then senior manager. She was on the path of becoming one of the many partners there when she realized that it wasn't where she was supposed to be. She said, "It just wasn't the right fit for me and I knew I wanted a change. I stepped out of my comfort zone and took a chance. I applied and accepted a job at Midland Press, just a short month after having this realization."

As Ginny advocates in her classes and leadership programs, she looked to outside sources to discover and get clear on her life purpose. She's also withdrawn for deep reflection in vision quests for four consecutive years in the mid-1990s, another key to reinforcing her life purpose. Ginny heard about the vision quest concept through a mentor who lived in Portland. The mentor previously led the events, having participated in the past and becoming passionate about being someone to lead others through the process.

During the quest, Ginny spent two and a half days in a mountainous area by herself in deep self-reflection, disconnecting and meeting the requirement to not read or eat or connect in person with anyone (other than the leader who stopped by twice daily to check on her well-being). Every year Ginny completed the vision quest was a different experience. She said, "One of the years was right after I lost one of my dogs, the next year was six months after I lost my mother, so every year had different things going on. There were a couple of years where I was crying a lot, which was good. You need to get that out of your system. The last year I did it, I wasn't crying. The quest was actually very positive." As she sat in reflection during those four days in late August, Ginny let what popped in her head come in, agreeing to be quiet and listen to her purpose to deepen her connection with Spirit.

One thing that became clear to Ginny on her first quest pertained to her relationship with joy. She said, "Somewhere in my life I developed a limiting belief that if I had too much joy—if I had too many good things in my life—that something bad was going to happen as a result. Reflecting back, I can remember times when I've held myself back, worried that I might be having too much fun, for fear of the bad that might happen. That limiting belief—that fear—also prevented me from having a stronger relationship with Spirit." Realizing that bad things and setbacks are going to occur inevitably because that is what life is about, Ginny decided to allow as many good things into her life as possible to make any bad things pale in comparison, thereby eliminating that limiting belief, allowing her to fully step into the leadership role right for her.

Leadership is a word found at the center of Ginny's life purpose. It is not only what she is herself, but it is what she fosters in everyone with whom she works. For years, she has used the Center for Character Based Leadership's (characterwork.com) definition that "Leadership is the ability to create a compelling vision of the future and then having the talent, heart, stamina, and focus to bring it to life." According to Ginny, leadership is about creating a vision for the future. "But in order to take action and bring that vision to life, we need to tap into our entire being: our talent comes from our head, our heart from our heart, our stamina from our body, and our focus from our spiritual grounding. Absent any of these, we will not be the best leader we can be—and we won't be living up to our true potential in life."

An initial step to becoming clear about your life purpose is to discover your strengths; strengths which, many times, you can leverage to handle any obstacles that come your way. To discover your strengths, Ginny advises simply interviewing people you know—personally and professionally. Ask them, "Will you please tell me about a time when you've seen me at my best?" Listen carefully to their examples, ask them for more, and look for patterns.

Ginny's core talents and strengths are influencing others and having a desire to develop people, which is the main offering provided in her business. When she realized these were her core talents and strengths, she looked back at the times even when she was in college or at her previous position and found that the things really made her happy were when she was working in helping other people develop their leadership skills. She said, "That was where it became very clear that was my passion. I was good at it and wanted to continue. The clarity of my passion and what I am truly good at and want to continue to get better at are definitely what drove me."

Therefore, another way to discover your passion, strengths, and purpose is through your own personal reflection. Think about the days when you seem to be most energized about your work, when you seem to lose all sense of time, or when you notice you feel more energized when you leave than when you arrived. Those are all cues of times when you are working out of your strengths.

A third way to discover and celebrate your strengths is to read the book *Strengthfinder 2.0* by Tom Rath, which also includes an online assessment. The assessment identifies your five core talents together with suggestions for putting those talents to use. The unique code for your online assessment is included on the jacket of the book. In the Strengthfinder test, a few of Ginny's top strengths were woo (meeting people and making connections), activator (taking action and reacting), and responsibility (being dependable and getting things done).

The final step after gaining the knowledge is to reflect and be sure you are working in areas of your strengths. That might require you to have conversations with your boss, supervisor, and/or family or to change the way you are approaching things.

Ginny recognizes that probably one of the biggest struggles for a lot of people is that they don't know their passion and they have trouble figuring out what that is, despite the recommendations above. That's why it is a big part of what Integrity Integrated does in its leadership classes: spending time helping people understand what they have done, what they like to do, and what they are passionate about. "I work with people to create purpose statements for themselves. The purpose statement includes what they're passionate about, what their values are, and what kind of work they really do want to do. It's hard for people to give themselves credit for what they're good at and truly figure out what they're passionate about."

Sometimes people don't get clarity on their purpose statement and that's tough. There are different reasons for this. For some people, it's just hard to get clarity about their passions. They may realize they're not in the kind of job they want to be in, or that it's hard to change what they are doing, even if the change is to pursue their passion. Some will not spend a lot of time working towards figuring out their purpose because the work that needs to be done may seem too difficult. They realize they are too far away from where they want to be and don't want to take the steps to move. They may not want to upset friends, families, or co-workers to make this change. Instead of changing, they keep doing what they are doing, even if they are unhappy. Change is hard.

You must believe you have the power to change; if you don't, then you aren't likely to set aside the reflective time to discover your purpose and create a personal vision for your future. To help deal with this prospect of change in your life, Ginny created these guidelines, which will walk you through some important questions to better gauge your grounding and readiness for change.

Change: Do I view change as positive or negative? Am I proactive or reactive when it comes to handling change in my life?

Vision: Do I have a written five-year vision for the future?

Balance: Where do I take time for myself—time to re-energize and make myself a priority? Am I spending time and energy on the important areas of my life?

Purpose: What's my clarity of purpose? Am I using my gifts and talents to create positive change for a cause that I'm passionate about?

Responsibility: Where do I assume the role of victim in my life? How can I step into 100% responsibility? What's my capacity to ask myself? What can I do to make a difference in the situation?

To Ginny, an effective leader is when someone is helping create positive change, whether in their department, company, or community; effective leadership is about creating effective change.

Therefore, following your passion and becoming clear about your life purpose can have an indirect impact on the world. Often when people get clarity, some do want to do things that help the community or take on projects to better develop the world. But to be great leaders, they don't have to set out to change the world. If everyone was truly working on being an effective leader in their own way according to their own passion and purpose, it would change their company, department, or even just their own world, which would create a positive impact on the community and the whole world.

Ginny defines the word, "leader," widely and she believes that anyone can be a leader. However, it doesn't mean leaders have to have direct reports, because sometimes their passion is not to develop other people. They might be an effective leader in their own way but it doesn't have to be in an official leadership title.

It's possible that you may fulfill your passion and life purpose with different endeavors. For Ginny, that's teaching, including for the Master's of Business Administration (MBA) programs at the University of Iowa. She said, "Teaching gives me energy. I enjoy getting to work with people who are truly interested in developing themselves. I get personal satisfaction helping others understand their strengths and their passion. Even though I often work long hours, I won't be tired because when I do things I truly love, it's not draining to me. It's exciting! Teaching is motivating to me. Yes, I sometimes get physically tired—there are occasional times when doing so much during a week and literally everything I'm doing are things I'm passionate about, but I can overdo with how many things I put in there. Sometimes we overwhelm ourselves."

Ginny has found energy even when teaching in less traditional situations. One December, she taught a leadership course in a compressed format where the class met over four weekends: three hours on Friday evening and eight hours on Saturday. About this experience, Ginny said, "I found myself driving home at the end of the weekend feeling more energized than I dreamed possible. The group of 58 students was highly engaged—and I was in my element—teaching to highly motivated people—that experience was one of my best."

Updated Reality –2018

Greg and I are still living in our dream house in the country. We had to say goodbye this year to both of our beloved dogs, Grace and Sam. We spent our 20-year wedding anniversary in Jamaica.

My work is still what I described in the vision. I continue to teach MBA classes, including an executive MBA class in Hong Kong and Italy as well as in Des Moines, Cedar Rapids, and Davenport, Iowa.

Integrity Integrated has a staff of two people in addition to me. They handle all of the marketing and communication work. We are active on social media websites such as Facebook and Linked In. We send out a monthly newsletter and I often will record a video message to post. I encourage my staff to get involved with non-profit organizations that speak to their passions and give them the time to volunteer. The greatest joy I get from my work is seeing the change in those I am privileged to work with whether it is one on one coaching, leadership groups, or MBA classes.

Ginny with her family in 2018

As with all leadership journeys, the road isn't always smooth and sunny, there will be bumps along the way. Ginny's journey has been no exception.

STORIES AND ADVICE ABOUT FINDING CLARITY

Ginny is my Gandhi by Kelly Burich
Virbac

How many of us can throw out our personal "leadership" mantra or coach's wisdom? Probably many. While the great notables may see all of the press coverage, for me, just a commoner in industry, my "Gandhi" of leadership is Ginny Wilson-Peters.

I've always been a bull in a china shop. I don't understand or relate to those who explain why they "can't." I don't think my intent has been to honk everyone off in my effort but realizing my own strengths and weaknesses in leadership came about by way of Ginny. Another friend recommended Ginny's "Women in Leadership" series, and it took my BICS (since we have to acronym driven in today's hipster society... that's short for "Bull in China Shop") strengths to the next level, and helped me realize that leadership isn't so much about bulldozing.

Ginny helped me get to the root of my "why"—why did I want to pursue other options? How would I inspire those around me? What would I do differently? Better? Smarter? How would I facilitate change? The bonding she created in a team of women opened my eyes to so many truths in leadership that I'm still exploring. How do we continue to push against the glass ceiling? What can we achieve, even in spite of fear? Our WIL (again....hipster code for "Women in Leadership") team created what I consider to be my mantra learned from Ginny: "Go. Go Afraid, but Go."

Through Ginny, I've committed myself to inspire other women. Ginny has coached me on what I put out to the universe and how to get it to come back to me. Every five years, my cartoon roadmap is updated and placed upon my past cartoon roadmap. If you've been through this exercise with Ginny, the significance is understood. Ginny helped me combine my childlike spirit into a source of spirited, positive development through my roadmap. She's coached me on how to achieve my goals and dreams, personally and professionally. And, as she's quoted me in the past, Ginny's commitment to and style of leadership coaching has made me want to grow to be better and to do better, at home and at work.

Ginny has shown me the relevance of all of buzzwords: Emotional IQ, Vulnerability, Dancing on the Glass Ceiling. But what will stay forever with me is "Go. Go Afraid, but Go"—it's okay to be scared. It's okay to be vulnerable. It's okay to be uncertain. But you cannot achieve if you stay compounded by your fears or your self-proclaimed inadequacies. She's my annual reminder to not set resolutions, but to frame my expectations. Leaders go. They go afraid. But they go.

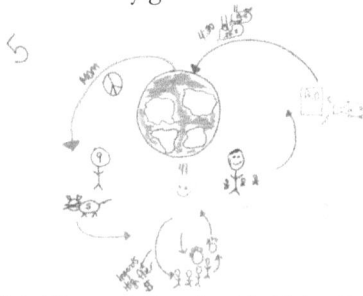

Kelly's Women in Leadership Vision Exericse.

Finding Passion to Thrive by **Kelly Hendershot**
Gilda's Club

Unfilled. Unpassionate. Uninterested, even. These were thoughts invading my mind regarding my job at an online company targeting the newspaper industry. I had loved this job and created the marketing department. But on a Wednesday evening in 2008, something wasn't right. I asked Melissa Wright, "What do I have to do to be you someday?"

Melissa was facilitating a caregivers' support group at Gilda's Club, allowing us to discuss our emotions with others as our loved ones were living with cancer. My husband, Justin, was attending a separate support group for those with a cancer diagnosis.

Cancer had shifted my priorities in an irreversible way. I realized in observing Melissa that I was lacking passion at work.

After Justin's death in 2009, I asked Melissa my question again. She became my mentor as I pursued my Master's in Social Work (MSW) in 2010, a decision that baffled many. I couldn't articulate it well, but it felt right. It also gave a spark to my life as I tried to keep my head above water during my grief.

I started subbing for groups after earning my MSW in 2013. A year later, I was part-time. But when I was offered a full-time position in 2015, I almost said no.

By then, I was VP of Project Management at a credit union. Could I afford the change? Was I ready? Perhaps the biggest question, would I be happy?

On July 1, 2015, I started full-time at Gilda's Club. I

have absolutely no regrets and continue to say yes to new opportunities that fuel my passion. In April 2018, I followed Melissa's footsteps by stepping into the Program Director position. After nearly 20-years, it was her time for a change.

If not in our careers, we need to find happiness and passion elsewhere to really thrive. For me, what started as a desire for passion has turned into a beautiful way to live on in Justin's memory.

Leadership in Non-Profits by LuAnn Haydon
Retired, John Deere

When I think of leadership, words like respect, honesty, confidence, commitment, integrity, and trust come to mind. These words now define me and live in all aspects of my life.

I have always embraced and admired those who motivated me to act. . . sometimes at a level higher than what I felt possible. I was born into a family where my benchmark was led by two of the strongest women I know, my grandmother and my mom. In their everyday walk in life, they showed me the way to lead through personal giving and service.

I feel blessed with my wonderful career at John Deere. It offered many diverse opportunities and challenges that not only built my character but filled my toolbox of knowledge and experience. I knew that the riches of those experiences could be my platform to assist young women in our community to also see that it is possible to reach for those benchmarks that will set them apart and provide opportunities beyond what they may see for themselves.

I have always been an advocate for women, children, and those impacted by cancer who need not only my help, but the help of many agencies within our community that afford the support they need. Because of that advocacy, I have been drawn to local organizations that address those needs. Over the past 20+ years, I have supported those agencies with my time and experience to build on their assets, bring in financial and physical support for their sustainable future, and work in whatever fashion they need to bring awareness to their organizations.

In most recent years, my focus has been directed to newly formed not-for-profits. My volunteer time has been spent leading strategic planning and board orientation sessions, formulating and conducting focus groups for growth and development, mentoring young professionals, and even chairing an inaugural fundraising event for one of the agencies. Currently, I serve on the Board of Directors for four local non-profit agencies. These last four years have been some of the most remarkable and inspiring years of my community-oriented life.

By being present for the women who will become the next leaders in our community, I truly feel I'm doing what my life experiences have trained me to do. I believe it comes with my time to continue to be there, to have those conversations, to introduce them to our community assets (the people, places, and opportunities), and to empower them to discover their potential. It's what I do and who I am.

OVERCOMING OBSTACLES

As with many things in life, the path to success isn't always a straight line and can take some twists and turns. Ginny became the Chief Financial Officer at Midland Press; three and a half years after being in this position, she took a 360-degree leadership assessment where her colleagues and direct reports reviewed her. She received eye-opening feedback.

On the positive side, Ginny received reinforcing feedback about her intelligence as well as a desire to lead and motivate people to do well and develop themselves. On the other side, Ginny received feedback saying she was cold, unempathetic, judgmental, arrogant, abrasive, and too hard on people, but the one thing that stuck out the most was that she was a stress breeder. She said, "As I read this report, I had an image come to my mind of what was going to be engraved on my tombstone. 'Ginny Wilson Peters – Stress Breeder.' That was a defining moment in my life, and I knew I needed to make changes. I accepted this feedback and realized that I needed to change. I focused on developing myself as a leader by reading a lot on the topic, attending many leadership events, and I started working with a coach."

As she was working on herself as a leader, Ginny took on a new role. In the early months in her role as President of Midland Press, she considered it her job to help other people behave like her. She said, "Sad, but true. I assumed that since I had been successful to date and taken on the role of President at the age of 34, then surely other people should strive to be like me. Thank goodness I discovered otherwise."

Ginny realized her role as a coach is to help people develop their strengths and become the best they can be. "Not the best person I want them to be—or their spouse or parents or children or their boss want them to be. Rather, it's about stepping fully into the person they were put on Earth to be."

She started to do a much better job working with her direct reports and their teams. While in this role, working with her coach and improving herself, she gained clarity on her purpose: to nurture and inspire others to reach for the stars. In fact, in 1998, Ginny was named one of the Top 40 under 40 Presidents in the printing industry by the professional association that governed the industry.

Ginny also realized that to fulfill her purpose, she needed and wanted to start her own business, which would require her to eventually leave Midland Press. When she gained clarity on her purpose, Ginny originally thought she would stay at Midland Press for four to five more years; though it wasn't completely fulfilling her passion, she liked what she was doing and wanted time to prepare for her new venture.

But some changes were happening at Midland Press. One day, the owner sat her down and said, "Ginny, I would like you to start buying into ownership of our Midland Press Corporation and eventually take over 100% ownership."

Ginny said, "This was a tough situation to be in. I knew it was an amazing opportunity, but I also knew it was not where I wanted to go in my life. I told him I wanted to think about the offer before making any decisions." She spent a month analyzing, praying, and talking to her husband, Greg. At the end of that time, she had reinforced what she had already decided: she didn't want to do it.

She went back to the owner and said, "This is an awesome opportunity, but I need to let you know that at some point, I'm going to leave and start my own business." Starting her business then became something inevitable in her near rather than distant future, as her timeline was expedited. Ginny's boss knew her heart wasn't in it, and he wanted to bring someone else into her role so they could learn to do her job.

It was tough for Ginny to be at Midland Press during this time; she had originally had a great relationship with her boss, but her decision and subsequent difficult conversation strained it. But if she was going to live her purpose, she knew she must follow through.

After a strained few months, in February, the company owner sat her down and said, "Okay, you are done. This is your last day. You are leaving." Ginny said, "I was already planning to leave; however, I wasn't planning to officially be let go, which is what happened. It was a very emotional time for me. Only two years after writing my five-year plan, I was going to start putting purpose into action. This is when I started Integrity Integrated."

STORIES AND ADVICE ABOUT OVERCOMING OBSTACLES

Do Things That Scare You by **Lindsay Hocker** **WQPT**

One of the biggest lessons in leadership I have learned is that it comes in many forms, so never feel like you have to fit a certain mold to be successful. You do not have to be fearless, but you do have to be present and determined.

To help myself grow, I challenge myself to do things that scare me. You can't grow if you just keep doing what you have always done, and taking risks means acknowledging the possibility of failure. You might fail when you push yourself, but I have found you are much more likely to succeed.

As a shy kid, I probably wouldn't have believed what I was capable of if someone told me about my career path. Being a news reporter required constant interactions, high-stress situations, and competing deadlines, and yet somehow, I loved it.

I eventually pursued new opportunities and moved on to the nonprofit field. Finding places to grow with missions I believe in has been key for me in my leadership journey, and I feel so fortunate I have been able to positively impact my community while serving at each organization.

Leading by example might be overlooked by some, but it is so significant. My best piece of advice is to invest in people at work and at home, including yourself. Part of that investment is staying true to your values and realizing you are capable of great success when faced with opportunities and challenges.

Leadership and a Polo Shirt by Melissa Pepper
Total Solutions

Our workplace is pretty casual, so most days the IT team wears jeans. HR purchased polo shirts for everyone to wear when visiting clients. One of the members of my team immediately started wearing his frequently. The other member had his for weeks and hadn't worn it once. HR came to me and asked if I knew anything about why this team member wasn't wearing his polo shirt. Being new, I had no idea. But I caught myself thinking, *Why the heck isn't he wearing this free polo shirt we gave him? He must be trying to send a message. He probably hates us.*

The HR manager revisited with the team later in the week and asked everyone how they liked their polos, if they fit, if they wanted other colors, and so on. Everyone seemed relatively pleased. The non-polo-wearer chimed in with, "They need a pocket."

He went on to explain that he likes to keep his phone in his shirt front pocket. Without a pocket, the polo was useless to him. Did he hate us? No? Was he trying to send a passive-aggressive message to us? No. He simply needed a pocket for his phone.

With this revelation clearly explained, we were off to order a few pocketed polos.

Problem solved.

Sometimes, all we need to do is ask simple questions to find simple solutions.

Had we not invited conversation about the polos, we could have started to look for other non-existent clues leading us to why this team member hated his job and was probably burning parts of the polo shirt at home each night. Thankfully, this wasn't the case at all.

Too often, I find myself sinking into worst-case scenario thinking. The polo pocket reminds me to ask questions and refrain from making assumptions. What is the polo situation in your workplace? As leaders, it's not our job to know all the answers, but we are called to ask the right questions and help our team (or ourselves) find the "pocket" solution.

Lead by Example by Mikael Gibson
Black Hawk College

In my years of leadership, I have learned that much of being a strong leader is about the ability to allow people to see their role in the larger project. It is very easy to get isolated in your own corner of the world and not realize how or why the things you do affect yourself or those around you.

In my first management job, we had a time management system that required my staff to document every segment of their day in quarter-hour increments. In a work environment where the focus of their time was counseling women and children in crisis, paperwork was low on the staff's priority list. It also lacked the level of detail necessary to illustrate the wonderful work that they were doing. As a counselor, I understood their focus being on the client, as it should be. As the current supervisor and grant writer, I knew that this system of time documenting in paperwork did not allow us to show our funders all the amazing work that was being done with our clients.

I decided to lead by example. To show the line workers why documentation was so important, I gave them the opportunity to attend the monthly funders meetings. This was also how I learned to understand the importance of paperwork.

At the state meetings, they heard the funder talk first-hand about how funding areas would be reduced because advocates were not utilizing it across the state. Each of those workers came back to the office with a different understanding of how a small adjustment on their part made a large impact of what kind of funding would be impacted at a state level. With that level of understanding, each of them returned to work advocating to their coworkers how important the quality of the paperwork was, providing a much higher investment in quality paperwork than I would have gotten by complaining about the quality at weekly staff meetings.

STEPPING UP, STEPPING OUT

The world is a big place, and it's easy at times to feel lost and insignificant. To remind herself and others of the differences we can all make, Ginny often uses this story:

One day, an old man was walking along a beach that was littered with thousands of starfish that had been washed ashore by the high tide. As he walked, he came upon a young boy who was eagerly throwing the starfish back into the ocean, one by one.

Puzzled, the man looked at the boy and asked what he was doing.

Without looking up from his task, the boy simply replied, "I'm saving these starfish, sir."

The old man chuckled aloud, "Son, there are thousands of starfish and only one of you. What difference can you make?"

The boy picked up a starfish, gently tossed it into the water, and turning to the man, said, "I made a difference to that one!"

So, in the end, whose responsibility is it for putting your life on the path to fulfilling your passion and life purpose?

Ginny regularly tells another personal story to demonstrate this rationale. One day while walking back to the office, she observed a child who threw a fast food bag out of a car window as it drove past her. As she watched it roll and settle on the side of the road, anger grew inside Ginny. How dare that child litter? How dare that parent or adult inside not turn around and make the child pick up the litter? But as she walked past, she thought about how dare she leave the litter there, especially since it bothered her so much? Whose responsibility was it for the litter being there, anyway? Was it the child's? Was it the adult in the car for not teaching the child properly? Or was it Ginny's for passing it by? Ginny returned to the litter, picked it up, and disposed of it properly.

Taking your life in the direction you want it to go is ultimately your responsibility, and it's ultimately your choice. You can choose to allow the obstacles you'll inevitably face stop you and make you turn back from living your best life, or you can choose to face them.

After understanding your passion and life purpose, the next key to stepping fully into your leadership destiny is to be willing to take risks, step out of your comfort zone, and do the kind of work that you truly want to do. Ginny had to step out of her comfort zone to start her own business. She said, "Starting your own business may be very scary for some people because of the income or lack of income. I tell people they need to be careful not to try to do everything. One of the things that worked for me was to connect with those in my network and meet new people to help me create core marketing pieces. My coach at Midland Press did leadership development work in Minnesota. She shared information with me about what she did, so that when I started my business, I didn't have to create everything from scratch. I was able to bring in some she used to help me get started."

The key for Ginny is that she wants people to know what they're passionate about and to live their best life personally as well as professionally. Sometimes your passion won't align with what other people in your life want you to do. Ginny advises, "Follow your heart; your heart is your passion."

To help prepare you to step out of your comfort zone when you need to, it can be helpful to write down your vision for a future date, as Ginny did back in 2002 for 2007. Knowing what you need to do can sometimes give you the courage you need. Put that future date in your calendar, and then get out your vision to see how what happened stacked up.

As you saw at the beginning, Ginny's life didn't exactly follow the vision she created five years previous. But she didn't expect that it would. She said, "You see, it isn't about creating a vision that you have to accomplish exactly. But it is about dreaming big, writing down those dreams, and revisiting them often to make sure you're on the path to creating the life you want to live."

Stepping out of your comfort zone sometimes means finding grace in things not turning out the way you would want them to. One winter, Ginny saw an ad in *Fast Company* magazine looking for the top 25 women business owners who have made a difference in this country through their work. Her first thought was, *Hey, I am going to apply for that award.* When she went to the website and began completing the application, doubt began to creep in. Some of the questions asked how many employees the company had, what kind of progressive policies were in place (who has policies?), and other questions that made it appear that they were looking for women heading up much larger companies. But she proceeded anyway with the confidence that the work she was doing at Integrity

Integrated was, in fact, worthy of recognition with other women business owners. Ginny didn't win the award, but she said, "The process of completing the application was very empowering as I thought about all the differences we'd made in the lives of men and women through our six-plus years at Integrity Integrated, Inc."

Though starting a business took Ginny out of her comfort zone, at least a bit sooner than she'd expected, she wasn't exactly scared. She knew she would be starting to do what she was meant to do. She said, "I mean, it was scary to leave a position I was good at, a steady income, and the comfort of the routine, but I knew it was time. I was ready to start to live my life fully dedicated to my purpose. I knew that Integrity Integrated was it. My husband was a huge support to me and stuck by my side whenever I had doubt."

The first groups through Integrity Integrated were women only, and she continues to host female-only leadership programs that meet for an entire year. As she expanded, she also developed a co-ed leadership program. She's found that women still face the obstacle of having a harder time moving up in many organizations. Women, in general, are harder on themselves than they should be. She said, "If there's an opportunity for advancement in their company, women will make sure that they have 80-90% of the skills needed for that position, whereas men will tend to apply even if they are only 50% qualified. So, I remind women that we don't have to be overly qualified to apply."

When stepping out of your comfort zone, it's important to develop a trust in yourself and a belief that everything will work out for the best in the end. Ginny learned this through her own experiences as well. One time, she gave a presentation on effective influence tactics at the Illinois Governor's Workforce Conference. In her final preparation, she struggled to find an example for one of the principles, the Principle of Scarcity, which says that when we remind people of the scarce availability of an opportunity, they will often be influenced more quickly to make a decision to change. The evening before the presentation, Ginny decided not to push it and to trust that the story would somehow present itself.

The next morning, the room began filling up quickly, and at five minutes before the start, there were limited seats available. By the time the presentation started, it was standing room only. Ginny realized the Principle of Scarcity had told its own story right there in the room. It seemed that as they approached the starting time, and seats became more and more scarce; there were more and more people trying to get into the room.

When Ginny reached that part of the speech, she simply reminded the participants what happened at the beginning of the session.

Related to the Principle of Scarcity is the Law of Abundance, about which Ginny also realized something that day. When she lives in recognition of her connection with Spirit, the universe is there to support her with abundance. She trusted her intuition and was presented with abundance—both in attendance as well as the scarcity story that unfolded. The same opportunity for abundance and connection exists for all of us.

In preparation for opening her business, Ginny reached out to a marketing company in the Quad City area. She sat down with them and they asked questions. Within that discussion, they came back and said, "It could be kind of a tough word to put out there, but based on what we heard, we feel like you should call your business Integrity Integrated." Ginny definitely resonated with that.

For the first leadership sessions, she created a clear document about what the session was about. She sent it out to many people but didn't hear back from anybody. Frustrated, she reached out to those same marketing people she talked with before to ask, "What's going on?"

They said, "You can't just wait for people to call you. You need to reach out to people you know." That's where they helped Ginny to realize that when you start a business, you can't just put it out there and wait for business to come to you, you must reach out to other people. They helped to name the business and helped Ginny truly connect with people. Ginny also took on the company's marketing responsibility.

Fast forward to fall of 2003 when Ginny had three different women ask her what she planned to do to market the company; two of the conversations were in person, and one was in a dream. One of those personal conversations was with Heather Pederson. Heather had been a participant in the Illinois Chamber Leadership Academy that Ginny co-facilitated. After completing the program, Heather invited Ginny to lunch and asked about her plans for the business for the next five years. She told Ginny that every time she had come home from a leadership academy session, she raved about Ginny's passion for her work. Finally, her husband, Ed, said to her, "Why don't you just invite Ginny to lunch and tell her you want to work for her?"

And so she did. Heather told Ginny that if her five-year plan included a marketing person, she wanted to come and work for Integrity Integrated. Ginny said, "Having Heather as part of this company in its infancy has been a tremendous boost to me and the company."

When Ginny started the business, she allowed the

clients to dictate some of the topics she spoke about, even though it might not have been a topic Ginny was passionate about. Part of getting started meant that she sometimes needed to offer her services gratis to make connections. Once she was established, she was more comfortable referring clients to others when they requested topics that were not her passion.

Over the years, Ginny and Integrity Integrated have worked with many Fortune 500 companies in the Quad Cities, Cedar Rapids, and Des Moines. These companies have been very supportive of Integrity Integrated's leadership programs and customized training. With these companies and as individuals, Ginny has worked with thousands of participants through her leadership programs and luncheons in the Quad Cities, Cedar Rapids, and Des Moines. She has also impacted countless others through community speaking engagements and more.

Ginny knows she's been on the right path toward working according to her passion and life purpose because what she does continues to bring her energy. She said it brings her the most energy, "When a client has figured out what their passion is, and they develop themselves to be a better leader, which in turn helps them develop the company overall. The best compliment we get is when someone is referred to us."

Many of Integrity Integrated's clients come to the business from such referrals. In a recently started Women's Leadership Group, four of the women said that they had a co-worker who had participated in a past session who encouraged them to sign up for the program. These four women and the rest of the group have learned about their passions, developed themselves, and have created positive changes in their work and lives.

In addition, Ginny's clients inspire her just as much as she seems to inspire them. One such person is Randy Moore at Iowa American Water. Ginny said, "I have been working with him for many years and we continue to push each other to be our best selves."

Leadership is a journey, not a destination. Especially when starting a business from scratch. "I can't imagine just flipping a switch and it working immediately. It was helpful that I had the specific plan and vision starting this business. I made sure I was saving a lot of money at home, because I knew when I started the business, I wouldn't be earning as much. When people tell me that they are wanting to go in a new direction that may cause a decrease in income, I remind them to look at what they need to be saving now, so that they can make it happen in the future."

About the future of Integrity Integrated, Ginny said, "I love what I do here. I love going to other countries, like Hong Kong and Italy, and working with other people and organizations, for-profits, and non-profits. I love learning and helping people. I don't see myself or Integrity Integrated slowing down anytime soon!"

STORIES AND ADVICE ABOUT STEPPING UP AND STEPPING OUT

The 500 Club by Chelsea Hillman
University of Iowa

I have a lot to be grateful for after Integrity Integrated. In the almost five years that I worked with Ginny Wilson-Peters at Integrity Integrated, I built a foundation of self-awareness and confidence in my leadership skills, observed what it was like to be an authentic leader through not only Ginny's teachings but her words and actions towards me and others, and built lasting relationships with the most amazing and inspiring leaders in the Quad Cities, Iowa, and beyond! The leadership story I'd like to share with you is about how a group of elementary school girls reminded me of something I had forgotten.

While working at Integrity Integrated, we were encouraged to volunteer our time, talents, and skills with non-profit organizations near and dear to our hearts. It's through this opportunity that I found myself as a single twenty-something woman leading a Girl Scout troop which included two of my younger cousins. We were gearing up for the Girl Scout cookie sale and working through the curriculum about goal setting, creating a business plan, and practicing our sales pitches. For those of you who don't know, the Girl Scout cookie sale isn't just cute Girl Scouts showing up on your door to sell you some sweet treats, but it's the largest girl-led business in the world. This financial literacy program teaches girls about goal setting, decision making, money management, people skills, and business ethics.

As a troop leader with a few years under my belt, I knew what we had sold in the past and began talking to the girls about setting goals for this year. The girls were aware and very proud of the fact that through the cookie sale, they funded all our activities for the year. So of course, we started by talking about all the things they wanted to do. Horseback riding was always at the top of their list. Next, we began talking about how much those activities would cost and how many boxes of cookies the group would need to sell to fund our goals. The conversation continued with what we sold in previous years and asking the girls what individual goals they wanted to work toward this year.

As a Girl Scout myself, I remember going to my family and friends and asking them if they wanted to buy cookies. Each year I probably sold anywhere from 25 to 100 boxes. In the past, a few girls in our troop had set their sights on being part of the exclusive 500 club, which required members to sell at least 500 boxes of cookies, and they made it! We also had girls in our troop who were more like me and sold just to their family and friends. We were grateful for each and every box sold, so it made no difference to us how many boxes an individual girl sold.

This particular year, the girls were excited about all the activities that we had talked about, and in their enthusiasm to reach our goal, they started shouting out very ambitious individual goals. From my perspective, maybe a bit too ambitious. Many of the girls wanted to be part of the 500 club, and while it's a great accomplishment, I was also aware of how much work the girls had to put in selling door to door while also being involved in many other activities in their busy lives. It was a lot! Girl Scouts was important to them, but it was also just one of many activities the girls were involved in. I had clearly lost control of the conversation and began to think about how I could use the framework of SMART goals, like any good business woman, to talk to them about how these goals were great aspirations but how we could revise them to be more attainable and realistic based on the work involved and considering what we'd sold in the past.

Before I had a chance to gather my thoughts, the girls were throwing their hands in a circle and rallying around this big hairy audacious goal they had set. In that moment, I had a vision. In my vision, I was standing on a dock and my troop members were all getting on a ship. That ship was going to leave whether I was on it or not. It reminded me of a speech Ginny gave when she was accepting the Athena Award. She talked about how fearless little girls are, and she pondered when and how women lose the sense that we can do anything. In her speech, Ginny suggested it chips away the more we are told "no" or we "can't do that." I decided at that moment that I wouldn't be just another adult that told them "no," but I would support these girls on this journey. It wouldn't matter if we reached our goal or not because we would find greatness together along the way. That year, we not only met but exceeded our total troop goal.

Years later, I often think back to this particular meeting and how I felt in that moment. I like to think that group of elementary school girls reminded me of what it's like to be fearless and achieve great things. They taught me that while it's important to look at history, it's just as important to look beyond what we consider to be "realistic" and "attainable" to dream big. It reminds me of the story Ginny tells about when she decided to start her own business and seeing a painting with a woman standing on a cliff and a red shape just out of her reach over the edge. At the last moment, her heart became the wind. I like to think those girls, whether they will ever know it or not, helped me undo a few of the "no"s I've heard throughout my lifetime, and for that, I am eternally grateful. I also like to think that their experience will strengthen their self-confidence like armor so that future "no"s won't impact them as much. Because at the last moment, our hearts became the wind, and it was magnificent.

You Must Show Up by **Karen Dahlstrom**
Augustana College

I was 25, married, surrounded by supportive people, and working at my alma mater, Augustana College. I seemed to have my life together, but something didn't feel right. I wasn't clear on my career trajectory and questioned the impact I was having on my community. I felt like I could, and should, be doing more.

So, I quit my job and took a temp job at John Deere. I was in the middle of a quarter-life crisis, hoping I could change my path by starting over.

It was a risk, but ten years and three jobs later, the path actually led me back to Augustana as Executive Director of Admissions. But, I'm not the same person who left ten years ago. Today, I am more professionally fulfilled and civically engaged than I could have imagined. I've learned many lessons in my journey, and one stands out among the rest.

You must show up.

I don't mean show up to work every day (hopefully you do that already!). I mean show up where you find people who inspire you. Put yourself in places that create opportunities, and don't use life's busyness as an excuse not to show up. Everyone is busy, so it's really about priorities.

For me, it was making time to network. I attended leadership training sessions, went to lunch and learns, and set up meetings with old colleagues. I walked with co-workers at lunch. I signed up to volunteer with organizations I used to admire from the sidelines.

It took about three years for my quarter-life crisis to end, and to fully see that the risk was worth the reward. I firmly believe that a leader isn't someone with a title or a position. A leader is someone who has the courage to show up.

"Nothing Will Work Unless You Do." ~ Maya Angelou by Brandy Donaldson
Exelon Generation

My favorite poet, author, activist, and historical figure is Maya Angelou. We are both just little country girls from the sticks of Arkansas. When I was young, she was the greatest example of a famous person who I could look up to and see my own potential. Maya once said, "Nothing will work unless you do." Her wisdom was infinite. But those particular words were life-changing for me.

I've often faced adversity and uncertainty. But, albeit personal, private, or professional, I fall back to those words. Then I get to work. That advice has never failed me in career or life. My career has been a journey from news reporting to corporate communications management. I had to be willing to work very hard to make that leap. And through hard work, I've experienced career success.

I'm grateful for and fortunate in that area of my life. But my true passions are social justice and equality for all human beings. I consider it a personal commitment to uplift all who struggle to be themselves in all areas of life and society and to serve as a voice for those who are marginalized or often feel voiceless due to bigotry, inequality, or other social ills. That certainly requires work. It is a struggle. It's a fight. It's not always popular and can often be thankless. But when I fall back to Maya Angelou's words, "Nothing will work unless you do," I'm sustained and spurred on.

It truly is the best advice I've ever heard or read, and words I live by as an employee, an activist, an organizer, a community leader, and as a human being. And since there will always be work to do in the areas where my passions lie since I constantly seek to climb and improve, I can't imagine my life will ever be stagnant or boring. I imagine I will always find some work to do, as can we all.

We All Start Somewhere by Beth Grabin
QCR Holdings

This story starts about four or five years ago. At the time, I was the Controller of Rockford Bank and Trust, and I had just accepted a promotion that would move me back home to the Quad Cities. I recommended a promotion for one of my co-workers (Amber) to fill my prior position because I knew she had the background and drive to be successful in this role. Amber accepted this position, and since then, she has thrived! I couldn't be more proud of her growth and accomplishments.

About two years ago, I emailed Amber her bonus letter for the year and sent her a note thanking her for all that she does and congratulating her on a great year. Her response is what sticks with me. Her reply was very simply, "Thank you for giving me a chance." Those words made me think and reflect a great deal, even to this day!

When QCR Holdings first hired me 11 years ago, someone decided to give me a chance. And that chance changed my life forever. I found my dream job at a company that I believe in with all my heart. And that job helped me discover my passion for helping others to become leaders both professionally and philanthropically.

The purpose of this story is to remind you that we all start somewhere. And then someone "takes a chance" on us and lets us try something new and exciting. We grow, learn, and then do it all over again. That's the goal.

The only thing that can stand in our way is confidence—confidence in ourselves and our abilities. Too often, we don't believe enough in ourselves to take the next step. We tell ourselves we're not worthy enough, not smart enough, not "enough."

Here are three things that you can do to help yourself and others along their leadership journey:

1.   Give a chance—help someone realize their potential. We all know someone who we believe in. Encourage them to apply for that job or leadership position! Give them the reassurance that they ARE capable of taking that leap.

2.   Take a chance—do something that is out of your comfort zone. Apply for a job that's slightly out of your reach. Apply for a leadership position within a nonprofit.

3.   Say thank you to someone who has given you a

chance—it will mean the world to them.

We are all in this together, so the more we help each other, the better off we will be, both individually and collectively, which in turn will help our community thrive and be successful.

From Crew Member to Shift Manager by Mary McCumber-Schmidt
Trinity Health Foundation

I was 15 when I accepted my first "real" job. I was hired as one of the original crew members of the Pizza Hut in my small community. I remained at Pizza Hut throughout my high school years, and it was the place I returned to during college breaks. It was there that I learned an important lesson that has become the foundation of the style of leader I strive to be. I have come to know that lesson as "participatory leadership."

Participatory leadership means to me that a true leader never asks or expects someone else to do something they themselves either haven't done or wouldn't be willing to do. Pizza Hut, and more specifically, Dan Sacco, who was my first "boss," modeled this for me on the nights we had to clean the pizza ovens.

Cleaning pizza ovens was the worst task imaginable. It was hot, greasy, and always occurred late in the evening after closing. Dan, in his white manager's shirt, worked beside us, guiding and directing us while being careful not to do it for us. He was assuring and remained as committed to the task as he expected us to be until it was complete. It was then after the ovens were clean that Dan would send us home and begin his closing work that would keep him there later into the evening.

When I was 17 and a senior in high school, Dan saw something special in me and did the unimaginable…he promoted me to a Shift Manager position. Being the Shift Manager created an opportunity for me to lead, take ownership, and experience a higher level of responsibility. My career at Pizza Hut has long come to a close, but I attribute much of my success to the early teachings from Dan that have manifested themselves in a long career and amazing opportunities to provide leadership in the Quad City community.

A Personal Starfish Story by Denise Beenk
Vera French

A story that I identify with is "The Starfish," author unknown. For those unfamiliar, it is a story about a pile of starfish on a beach. A person comes along and throws the starfish back into the sea one by one, so they can survive. As an introverted leader, I identify with making the small, individual connection. I am a listener. I hear and understand the details important to others. I have been fortunate to find many others that find the value in these intimate connections as well. Many people have helped me achieve my vision of making a difference. Here is my starfish story:

This story is about Sheila, a young woman I worked with early in my career. Sheila was a young, single mother raising two children. She was living in a low-income housing project on welfare. When I first met her, she led me into her apartment. Her kids were running wild, she had run out of diapers, and there was garbage strewn all over. I worked with Sheila over the next year and connected her to mental health services. In working together, she learned how to plan, budget, use public transportation, and fill out benefits applications. I assisted her in getting a job, getting her kids into safe daycare, and becoming self-sufficient. I had the incredible opportunity to see her rise above her circumstances and successfully exit the welfare rolls.

Here's what I know: I made a difference to Sheila. And by making a difference to her, I made a difference to her children. These small changes impacted her family, her friends, her neighborhood, her employer, and her community. As a leader, I care about each starfish, because when you throw one back into the water, you create a ripple in the ocean.

Moving Toward by Ann McGlynn
St. Paul Lutheran Church and Founder of Tapestry Farms

The two poems Ginny Wilson-Peters gave me nearly a decade ago still hang on my bedroom dresser mirror. The corners are curled, the edges a bit torn up, but I refuse to replace them.

Their words ground me every single day. Here is one excerpt from "Everything Has a Deep Dream" by Rachel Naomi Remen:

In befriending life,
We do not make things happen
According to our own design.
We uncover something that is already happening
In us and around us and
Create conditions that enable it.

Everything is moving toward its place of wholeness
Always struggling against the odds.

Everything has a deep dream of itself and its fulfillment.

When I first got to know Ginny more than eight years ago in her Grow to be CEO course, life was pretty rough. I was emerging from a difficult divorce with two young sons. At the same time, I felt a pull to do something different professionally.

Ginny's wisdom and guidance set me on a course that I didn't always completely understand—but now can see clearly. She helped me recognize my courage to step away from comfort and into growth.

With encouragement from Ginny, this writer (journalists are not known for their math skills) enrolled in the University of Iowa Master's of Business Administration program. Ginny taught my first class. It took me five and a half years, but I graduated in 2017 with honors.

Meanwhile, I went to work for the Girl Scouts of Eastern Iowa and Western Illinois. I learned about building girls of courage, confidence, and character who make the world a better place.

And then I went to work for St. Paul Lutheran Church, where my understanding of seeking justice for the most vulnerable strengthened and solidified. It is at St. Paul I encountered a refugee family—a single mom with six kids resettled to America.

All the while, Ginny was there in the background. She offered encouragement, guidance, and honesty.

Several months ago, I sat across the table from Ginny at Downtown Deli in Davenport. I shared an idea for a nonprofit social enterprise. The mission is to empower and encourage refugee women in the Quad Cities in the areas of employment, housing, education, mental and medical care, and community.

Ginny indicated she wanted to financially support Tapestry Farms. She told me the amount. I cried right there over my sandwich and chips.

Ginny was our first donor.

It's been a long journey to reach for my stars, Ginny. But today, because of years of friendship, expertise, and support, Tapestry Farms is now a reality. And we will continue your work, specifically with refugee women, encouraging them to always move toward reaching for their stars.

No Woman/Man is an Island by Jackie Staron
River City Tire

I have been a manager for over 20 years in numerous industries and am now part owner of a company. I attended Ginny's Women in Leadership program, and I was honored to meet women from different backgrounds with different levels of management training. All women from different industries, and all looking for skills to lead a successful team forward.

Understanding yourself was the key element for me. What personality factors affect the way we interpret, interact, and plan was a major factor in the success to implement team strategies. Each personality will react, interpret, and interact differently, and I, as a manager, must "talk so they can relate to me" or, I, as a manager, can never lead a team. I was always told, "People don't think like you do" or "People don't work like you do," but

I forged forward, not always successfully. I felt like I was dragging my team instead of leading my team. With the assessments we did in the class, I not only learned about myself, but I learned to see how others interpreted situations and how I could use different language to achieve the results that would help the team be successful. Enhancing communication while utilizing team assessment points to ensure the team was moving forward.

I realized the reassessing and recommunicating were the jobs of the managers—let the team do their job. This helped improve employee engagement and responsibility to the mission, resulting in more job satisfaction.

I learned documentation of this process not only allowed for team assessment but helped identify those who were high achievers and those who needed assistance. Identifying those who were having or creating issues for the implementation of the plan and its success. Allowing individuals to be evaluated with concrete goal setting and engagement.

Each person—manager or employee—wants to know that what they do makes a difference in the operation of a company. Successfully using these processes allows them to achieve goals, not only for themselves but for the success of the team.

I realized also that "no woman/man is an island" even though I was brought up in the era of "we can do it all and have it all." There are always struggles, and therefore the need, to create a network of support is so important. To be able to reach out to other managers who struggle with the same issues who can assist or at least listen will help the leadership of tomorrow grow stronger.

Ginny listens while creating an atmosphere of learning,

engagement, and assessment. Helping others be better leaders, but more importantly, better people.

BUILDING A NETWORK

Having a supportive person and an extended network of supporters is also very important to fulfilling your passion and life purpose. To Ginny, her husband, Greg, has been the foundation of her support throughout her journey. Greg knew what Ginny was passionate about and where she wanted to go. Sometimes the only thing holding ourselves back is ourselves, even when we have a strong support circle.

One day early in planning the business, after she had a bit of an emotional setback, Ginny talked to Greg about what she was experiencing.

He said, "Honey, I just want you to be happy. If we must get a smaller place to live, that's okay." Luckily, they never did have to move, but having that kind of support was really, really important for Ginny to keep on her path.

It was also important for Ginny to rely on a network in running her business, so she didn't have to do all the work alone. Ginny was just by herself for a few years, but when it became very clear that she needed and wanted a marketing person, she hired Heather Pedersen. After she had been with Integrity Integrated for three years, Heather's husband was transferred internationally. At that juncture, Ginny hired Erin Hemm as the marketing director. When she moved on, Ginny brought in Chelsea Hillman.

As Integrity Integrated was growing, it quickly became clear that they needed an administrative assistant to work daily tasks and help with marketing. One fateful day while grocery shopping, Ginny ran into Ann and Becky Lorentzen. Becky had just graduated from college, and Ginny mentioned to her and Ann about the new part-time position created. Becky took on the position for a couple of years and then chose to leave for a full-time opportunity. After Becky left, they hired Amy Kolner.

After five years, Chelsea was offered an opportunity to work in marketing in a large company. When she left to go to Allsteel in Muscatine, Ginny brought Shari Baker in as the Director of Marketing and Communication. Amy's scope of responsibility had evolved so she became the Director of Business Development. Having only seven employees in two positions over twenty years is a testament to the positive working environment at Integrity Integrated.

The entire past and present marketing team at the Integrity Integrated 15th-anniversary celebration in 2014.

Not only do you need people supporting you in your endeavors, but it's also important to find people to look up to and inspire you in your leadership journey. Two main coaches have had and continue to have an impact on Ginny's life and career. They have helped her determine her strengths and things to work on.

Ginny's first coach was when she was the manager at Midland Press due to the feedback in her 360-degree assessment. This coach helped Ginny understand her strengths as well as things that she needed to work on to improve. After working with the first coach, Ginny could see the value of having a coach and mentor. She still works with her second coach, Alex Merrin, who had led Ginny on her vision quests in Portland.

Support networks are important, and for Ginny, they have expanded beyond just those closest to her. She wrote this article about gaining support from circles:

"Your Circle of Trust – A Place to Breathe"

A campfire in the center. A camp counselor playing guitar. Counselors with names like Birch and Patches and Froggie. And a circle of girls belting out their favorite songs. Sitting in circle at Girl Scout camp is among my favorite childhood memories (yes, even better than the Girl Scout cookies). Many times, we would march to the campfire and begin with a ritual to remind us of the sacred space we were entering.

My early memories of campfires were perhaps the seeds of my passion for sitting in circle with other women. Circles are certainly not unique to Girl Scout camp; women and men have been sitting in circle for centuries prior to my experience.

I will admit, though, that after my Girl Scout years, I went for many years without experiencing the positive support and energy of a circle of women. I grew up as the only girl in a family with three older brothers. In my twenties and early thirties, I didn't appreciate the value of connecting closely with other women. About ten years ago, a friend gave me a book called *Circle of Stones: A Woman's Journey to Herself* by Judith Duerk. It is a book about the power of women coming together in a circle, and asks, "How might your life have been different if there had been a place for you, a place for you to go to be with your mother, with your sisters and your aunts, with your grandmothers, and the great- and great-great-grandmothers, a place of women to go, to be, to return to, as woman? How might your life be different?"

Reading *Circle of Stones* re-ignited my earlier passion for circles. And I took action. Even before I left my previous job to start this company, I began inviting women to sit together monthly. Intuitively, I knew that we were to sit in circles. Our first circles met in my living room and we created our own rules for coming together. Many of those early rules are in place today—and they are consistent with the guidelines put forth by others for creating circle as a sacred space. When we moved into our current office space, we continued to pull the chairs together and sit in circle. Building code doesn't allow for a campfire at the center but we do have a place in the center with something representing each of the four elements: earth, fire, water, and air.

Over the years I have had the privilege of creating leadership circles for hundreds of women. Today we have seven different Women in Leadership groups that meet on a monthly basis. One group has been together for over seven years. Another is entering their third year. We also started a leadership program called Women's Leadership

Development in Cedar Rapids and Des Moines as well as the Quad Cities.

Why do women continue their commitment to these circles? Because the circle is a place where we can listen and learn and grow. Sarah, a woman in one of our leadership groups said the monthly meetings were "a place to breathe."

Teacher and cross-cultural anthropologist, Angeles Arrien, says there are four healing salves for our soul: song, dance, silence, and stories. Many of our circles encompass three of these four (with dance the one missing). I have seen women muster tremendous courage to approach personal change and/or professional change in their lives as a result of sitting in circle with other women.

*****

Whether you meet in circles or not, it's important to build a network of supporters. This can be difficult for some people, so here is a practical, step-by-step guide Ginny advises for building an extended network while also having fun:

1. Create and maintain a list of ten to fifteen people that you want to meet (internal and external to your organization). When you're meeting with your other alliances, look for connections between your current allies and people on your list with whom they can help you connect.

2. Create a personal board of directors. Identify 5-7 people whose opinions you value and establish a goal of having breakfast/lunch with them on a regular basis (quarterly for example). You don't actually bring your

"board of directors" together for a meeting, but these are people you know you can call when you're faced with an important decision in your career.

3. Set a goal for how many times a week you'll meet (breakfast, lunch, coffee, etc.) with people in your network.

Sometimes, your network will build you up so well that the tide may turn in the other direction so that you find yourself overwhelmed and overextended. Finding this balance can be very difficult, but it is key for continued success in growing your circles.

LEADERSHIP STORIES AND ADVICE ON BUILDING A NETWORK

Give People a Chance by **Regan Kunzman**
MidAmerican Energy

In the workplace, I tend to hear a lot of gossip, and people in positions of leadership make snap judgments about individuals based on a single interaction, or many times, at the word of another person they trust and respect.

About 15 years ago, I accepted my very first role in management. Of course, I had managed projects over the years, but now I was being entrusted to manage actual people….an entirely new challenge. My first order of business was to fill the role I had just vacated within the department I was now overseeing.

I really enjoyed all aspects of recruiting and hiring for this position. I had a strong pool of applicants and three out of the five interviews were very strong. But, without question, one person stood out among the rest. To me, hiring this individual required little mental effort on my part—she was by far and away the most accomplished and qualified applicant.

Upon announcing this promotion, though, I heard comments from my predecessor and my mentor like, "I think you'll regret that decision," and "She can be difficult to deal with." These comments have confounded me to this day because my subsequent eleven years with this person as my employee continually exceeded my expectations. To this day, I have never worked with a more thoughtful, dedicated, and intelligent person. She was eventually promoted out of my department into a position of leadership; she actually works for my previous mentor if you can believe that.

My point in telling this story is I think as leaders, we need to trust our instincts and form our own opinions about people. One experience or impression should not shape our entire career. Give people a chance, and they may exceed your expectations, too.

Do What You Say You Are Going to Do by Pat Shouse Trinity Health Foundation

I do not believe I possess any special leadership skills that separate me from the pack. Like many other leaders, I have an intense work ethic and a persistent focus on attention to detail. Toss in an obstinate passion to lift others up to their potential, and you have uncovered my secret. But I am certainly not alone in the high hopes of making a difference every day.

I feel blessed that I've met amazing people who have impacted my life throughout my career. Without knowing it, many were mentors for me. A mentoring relationship can be structured or unstructured, and mine were all unstructured—people who recognized my desire to grow and reached out to help me improve the circumstances around me. My husband, my friends, my coaches in sports, fellow board members, and my peers at work were all there to support and guide me. Because they helped me, I get to do the same for others. I push people to be forthcoming and sincere. I expect them to be honest and transparent. And above all, I insist they communicate effectively and then over-communicate some more. Work hard and always do what you say you are going to do. Then follow up.

I am very serious about the work I am responsible for. But I never take myself very seriously. I think laughter at work and home is a must. Plenty of other people can do what I do, I am just grateful I get the chance to do it. I am not special. I never ask of others what I am not willing to do myself. I never forget where I started. How we treat people is the true measure of one's core values and beliefs. At the end of the day, I hope that the great folks I work with and care about know how much I value them. I consider myself lucky when I get the opportunity to listen, coach, and help others be the best version of themselves.

We are all blessed to have a great friend and leader like Ginny who, through her work, has impacted so many people to be better leaders.

The Mentee Teaching the Mentor by Joe Slavens Northwest Bank

A few years ago, a very successful business owner asked me to mentor his son. I was flattered and honored that a person I respected so much thought his son could learn from me.

Prior to our first meeting, I read several articles about mentoring. I brought copies for him to our first meeting as well as some ground rules that I thought we should follow. At that first meeting, we discussed what he hoped to accomplish through our relationship and agreed to meet monthly.

During our first few lunches, he asked me questions. In response, I shared stories about my life experiences, both good and bad, and the lessons I had learned. I also asked questions, but mostly to provoke more questions from him. After just a few meetings, however, I now recognize that I started asking different kinds of questions, real questions about what he actually thought about issues I was confronting in my life. Many times, his answers reinforced what I already thought, but not infrequently, he had an entirely different take on things. I respected his answers because we share the same values, but I learned so much because the lens through which he interpreted our values and applied them to the facts was entirely different.

Several years into our relationship, I hope this incredibly bright, hard-working, and talented young professional still finds value in our monthly meetings. I have told him that I do.

So what have I learned?

• Each of us has more to learn than we do to teach.

• If you think someone is worth mentoring, they are also someone from whom you can learn, a lot.

• Everyone, at every age, can benefit from being, and from having, a mentor.

• Better yet, have more than one of each.

Grow to be CEO by Cheryl Goodwin
Covenant Health Network

Participating in Grow to be CEO was a game changer in my professional life. Ginny bringing a group of women together from all walks of life and career experiences to facilitate lessons and conversations around women in leadership was the group's purpose. However, what none of us bargained for were the lasting bonds that would be created amongst us, which extended far beyond the professional realm. Challenges that we faced as women leaders, fears that stopped us from achieving our best, balancing work and home, and obstacles to "Dancing on the Glass Ceiling" were the center of our discussions during the 90-minute, monthly sessions together.

Woven into those conversations were our personal struggles that hindered us from being the women we wanted to be outside of our professional roles. While I'm not sure Ginny realized the mix of women she brought together would have the magical connection that we did, she was instrumental in creating a safe environment in which we could explore our feelings, challenge one another (and ourselves), and champion each other. Our time together extended over a three-year period, growing from the core group to bringing in other professional women in a mentor/mentee structure. The more women leaders, the greater life lessons we were able to learn and grow from.

Professionally, I was promoted to a CEO position during the Grow to be CEO group; however, personally, I came out a stronger, more confident, insightful person and leader. My time with Ginny as our facilitator/leader and these wonderful women I met is a time professionally and personally, I will be forever grateful for. "Z Snap all the Way!!!!"

Thank you, Ginny!

A Better Community by Cheri Bustos
U.S. Representative for Illinois' 17th Congressional District

Selfless. Gutsy. Inspirer. Motivator. Candid with kindness.

Yep.

That's Ginny Wilson-Peters.

For years, Ginny would be the person I would turn to for career advice.

She would listen. She would guide. She would also push and pull—always with candor AND kindness.

In my family, we say it's only your friends who tell you the truth.

Ginny would always tell me the truth. Sometimes hard to hear. But necessary to hear. And helpful to hear.

I have had three careers in my life. Journalist. Healthcare executive. Congresswoman. Ginny has been there through it all.

I think the world of her. Especially because her North Star is helping others. She has helped me in countless ways. And she has helped so many others.

The end result has been the development of better leaders in our community. And, most importantly, a better community.

Thank you, Ginny

A Darn Good Swing by Beth Clark
Big Brothers Big Sisters

When I first met Ginny, she was President at Midland Information Resources. I was playing golf in her foursome that was a fundraiser for Junior Achievement. She was a good golfer. Not only a great swing, but her concentration and follow-through were very impressive.

When she started Integrity Integrated, she brought those same skills to her leadership development workshops and group facilitation. I became a member of one of Integrity Integrated President's Groups. In the beginning, the group consisted of eight of us who either owned or managed companies in the Quad City area. Our group was together for about two years. We met monthly at Ginny's office and were able to present situations to the group that we needed help on figuring out or making decisions about. Ginny helped us understand our "rules of engagement" with each other, helping us to understand that what was said within the group was in complete confidence and that we needed to actively listen to each other with open minds.

We operated like a private "board of directors," each having talents, skills, and experiences that were different from one another. We had each other's backs. It was comforting to know that these peers weren't there to judge you but to provide you with sincere support and ideas to help you. This group, guided by our gifted pilot, Ginny, helped me personally to make some of the most important decisions of my career. I am very grateful that Ginny put this group together and introduced me to these leaders who became my friends.

Ginny, I'm not sure how your golf game is these days, but I know how successful you've become, and I'm sure much of that success comes from your ability to concentrate and have great follow-through…not to mention a darn good swing. Thank you.

Leadership is a Relationship Between Individuals by Angie Kendall
Genesis Health Foundation

The one thing that has carried me through every success is relationships. The foundation of every single one of those relationships is a bedrock of trust built with honesty. Honesty with myself. Honesty with my team. Truth is my most powerful leadership tool.

What is my truth? What do I stand for? What do I stand against? What will I tolerate? If I don't know these things, I can't effectively lead. By connecting with my values, my truth, I can navigate hard conversations and make hard decisions. When choices become a matter of honesty and connecting with my values, those decisions, while not easy, make it easier to sleep at night.

Knowing and leading with my truth means that humility is a constant companion. I've never met a good leader who believes they have all the answers. In fact, every great leader that I admire admits they don't have all the answers. Which is why they develop diverse teams and build relationships with people who can inspire, engage, and teach them for a lifetime.

While intentionally surrounding myself with individuals who possess the very skills I lack so that I may grow, I must remember my commitment to them. My commitment to help them grow through honesty and trust. This means hard conversations. This means pushing them to reach their highest potential. This means trusting them when they falter; it means giving them the space and grace to explore. This also means building enough credibility that they trust me when I tell them to take the next step when I challenge them to do more.

Leadership is a relationship between individuals. There is no relationship without a connection. There is no connection without trust. There is no trust without truth.

BALANCING LIFE

Nobody's perfect. Even as far as she's come, Ginny still has things she's working to improve. The main one is work-life balance. Though she's been clear on the importance of work-life balance and encouraged those she serves to strive for it, Ginny admits, "I would not say I'm an example of work-life balance." Ginny believes that vacations and breaks are very important—without smartphones, computers, responding to emails, or doing anything for work. It's hard for a lot of people to disconnect like that, even Ginny.

In 2016, Ginny realized she needed to follow her own advice and totally disconnect. Even though she had been on family vacations every year for two weeks up in northern Minnesota, she always took her computer, responded to emails, and took care of any invoices that had to be created or payments to be made. This year would be different! She talked with Amy about taking on these activities while she was away.

She put a bounce on her email saying she wasn't going to respond since she was on vacation and to reach out to Shari or Amy with anything. It was the first time that she truly didn't do any work on vacation. It was a win-win-win for everyone because Ginny got to disconnect, and her team appreciated being able to help her do that. They also appreciated knowing that Ginny was confident in their capability for filling in.

Ginny and her family on vacation in 2018.

Burnout is a risk when you are truly living your passion and life purpose, so it's important to be aware and use vacations and time off when needed. Though Ginny has not experienced true burnout herself, she has noticed when things get too busy. When she commits herself too far, she steps back and takes some time to recharge. Ginny said, "I think there are many signs of burnout, and a lot of it has to deal with technology. People send so many emails and expect responses right away. It's hard for people to respond to everyone quickly. Because of it, it makes it hard for people to 'turn off' work when they need to recharge. The same thing is true for vacations. I've heard from many managers who will still call into work and check emails while they are on vacation, so people expect that to be the norm. That time is needed to truly disconnect so you don't experience burnout."

Ginny continues to strive to help everyone on her team work to create a work-life balance that works for them. At the beginning of 2018, she changed Integrity Integrated's time off policy, essentially eliminating a set number of sick, vacation, and personal days. Instead, she's empowered her employees to take the time they need, giving them the opportunity to get their work done in the office or at home, whichever works best for them. Ginny said, "I would say, overall, that's very positive because that gives them the flexibility to enjoy life and have a great work-life balance. They are engaged at work and are able to enjoy life." It's one of the reasons her employees nominated Ginny and Integrity Integrated for one of the "Coolest Places to Work" awards, which they won in 2015.

LEAVING A LEGACY

We positively impact the world one person or situation at a time, and people and leaders can make a difference in many lives in many different ways. Here's the reprint of a story Ginny wrote for one of her newsletters shortly after her mother passed away:

"Cake Lady...Bingo lady...Lover of bridge and card playing...Ceramic lady...Square Dancing lady in her younger years...Friend, Mentor, Sister, Grandma, Great Grandma, Mom, and Wife. We all had the privilege of experiencing Mom in different ways. And no matter what your experience was, you know the essence of Mom is love and unconditional giving to others."

On January 27, 2006, my mom died. Her passing came quickly for my family and me. I am thankful that I was with her at the hospital when she passed on. The above words were the first part of the tribute I wrote and spoke at her funeral.

Two days after Mom's passing, I sat with my dad, brothers, nieces, nephews, and great nieces and nephews and heard their stories. I also listened to friends and relatives who stopped by with food and to share memories. In the early days of grieving, those were bright spots for me.

Out of all the memories and stories was born the tribute: my attempt to capture Mom's essence and to celebrate her life during the funeral services. One of the ways Mom expressed her love and her creativity was through her cakes. Cake Lady was even her CB handle back in the days when we used CBs on the farm to communicate. When it comes to cakes, it goes without saying that the town of Colo, Iowa—and surrounding areas—couldn't REALLY celebrate a wedding, graduation, birthday, or another special occasion without a cake decorated by my mom.

And one of the things that I really appreciate about Mom's love for cake decorating was that she genuinely wanted to make a cake that was just right for the person celebrating. With the younger kids, it was usually a character cake like Barney, Mickey Mouse, or a Barbie Doll…or any of the other 200-plus character pans that Mom had. Because if she didn't have the character pan on hand and there was enough time to do so, she would order the cake pan just so she could please the young child.

And of course, she made cakes for all of us kids and the grandkids and great grandkids. All the grandsons grew up with John Deere tractor cakes for many of their early birthdays. Although, my nephew, Brandon, says he can still remember a year that Grandma made him a RED tractor cake instead of the traditional green. As we laughed about that, none of us could figure out a reason why she might have used red. It is interesting to note, though, that Brandon now works for Case Corporation. It's quite possible that Mom's intuition was working those many years ago. Or maybe Brandon was so intrigued by the red tractor that he just had to find out for himself what it was all about.

When Mom died, many people told us beautiful stories in tribute to her friendship and love. It made me wish that we had ignored my parents' wishes four years ago and thrown them a party for their fiftieth wedding anniversary. I wish that she had heard many of the tributes while she was alive, rather than after she passed. I know that I wish I had told her more often what I loved about her.

Ginny with her mom on her wedding day.

How often do we do neglect to tell others what we appreciate about them? From a leadership perspective, we know that people want to hear appreciation from their supervisor at least once every seven days. Personally, I want more—and I strive to express appreciation more frequently than that. In my groups and MBA classes, I often ask people if they have a file folder (hard copy and/or email) with thank you notes they've received. Over half the hands in the room go up. Yes, we all love to receive—and save—those words of appreciation and gratitude, so how about making a commitment to express your appreciation to others?

*****

Giving appreciation facilitates receiving appreciation, so Ginny advises making a commitment to yourself and setting a goal to express appreciation to another person every day. This can be done with a handwritten note, email, card, flowers, chocolate, or whatever creative way you imagine. It doesn't matter what form you use; what matters is that you take the time to let others know what you appreciate about them.

Ginny's mom and dad.

We impact people around us intentionally or unintentionally, and we have can have positive or negative influences on everyone with whom we come in contact. Finding your strengths, core values, passion, and life purpose and then consciously putting them into your life, taking action with the support of your network, overcoming obstacles, taking a risk, getting out of your comfort zone, and balancing all of it with self-care, can help provide the best chance that the impact you have as a leader will be positive. And remembering you don't have to impact change in the entire world, but just in one, will help keep you motivated to keep going.

ANOTHER STORY ABOUT
LEAVING A LEGACY

Everyday People Making Differences in Others' Lives
by Liz Terrill
Retired

When Ginny was my boss at Midland Press, she arranged for me to attend a week-long leadership training session in California. There I was exposed to leadership concepts that included the Drama Triangle, 100% Responsibility, and Authentic Communication, among many other topics—but in a California kind of way! I cannot begin to describe the paradigm shifts—or should I say overhauls—that the training triggered for me. Talk about game changers!

Ginny also encouraged me to determine my personal vision and calling. By serving that vision throughout my career, I have been blessed to work with many amazing people. How rewarding it has been to experience their personal growth and transformation, and to receive their support in my own.

Two of my favorite movies are *Mr. Holland's Opus* and *It's a Wonderful Life*. Toward the end of *It's a Wonderful Life*, Clarence says to George, "Strange, isn't it? Each man's life touches so many other lives. When he isn't around, he leaves an awful hole, doesn't he?" And in *Mr. Holland's Opus*, he is reminded to "Look around you. There is not a life in this room that you have not touched, and each of us is a better person because of you. We are your symphony, Mr. Holland. We are the melodies and the notes of your opus. We are the music of your life."

These movies speak to everyday people making differences in others' lives. Ginny has done that for me, and I hope I have adequately paid it forward. I celebrate the ripple of positive differences that I have directly and indirectly witnessed throughout my career.

Congratulations Ginny and thank you for your inspiration and support.

LESSONS FROM OTHER LEADERS

In addition to those stories from others whom Ginny has inspired to reach for the stars under the broad categories above, there are numerous additional stories below to continue to inspire and motivate you in your leadership journey.

Lead with Optimism by Steve Bahls
Augustana College

I've been thinking a lot about what it means to be truly engaged in a community. In a community like Augustana, our faculty and staff are actively engaged in advancing our mission of helping students grow in mind, spirit, and body. The Gallup organization has done extensive global research on what it means to be engaged in the context of the workplace. It defines engaged employees as those who "are involved in, enthusiastic about, and committed to their work—and who contribute to their organization in a positive manner." Engaged employees are the positive difference-makers in any organization.

I was surprised to learn that worldwide, only 13% of employees are engaged difference-makers. In the United States, the percentage is higher—about 30%.

So I urge you to decide now that you will be engaged in all of the communities of which you are a part—whether in the workplace, where you make your home or other organizations you love. I urge you to view the glass as half full, to see assets rather than deficiencies. If you do so, you will make a difference.

Of course, I am aware that some people write off engaged optimists as being blind to the problems in their workplaces or their communities. But my experience indicates the reality is otherwise. Effective optimists are fully aware of the limitations of their workplaces and their communities. They confront the cold, hard facts. In doing so, they have an abiding faith that, with commitment and hard work, limitations can be overcome for the common good. They focus on making their organizations and communities better and stronger by being more responsive to the common good.

My advice to you: Surround yourself with positive people. Fully engage with the here and now, not dwelling on past problems. Be realistic that there will be disappointments but look at these as opportunities for improvement. Be a life-long learner, so that you develop the tools to respond to change. Bring out the best in people. Focus on what you can control instead of what you can't. Use the power of critical thinking, but not simply to be critical, rather to be a creative problem solver. Let go of disappointments and be sure they don't cling to you. Have the optimism that allows you to have the tools to transform.

Learning from Others by Matthew DeBisschop
Ascentra Credit Union

I have the privilege of influential people in my life: parents, spiritual advisors, supervisors, community leaders, and my CEO, to name a few. Through serving as a human resources executive in the financial industry, I am fortunate in having the opportunity to collaborate and learn from these individuals on a regular basis. When you converse with someone of a caliber who flourishes at the top of their profession, it usually takes just five minutes to observe two things. First, they have a clear sense of self, accompanied by an unwavering passion for purpose. Two, they conduct themselves with the utmost levels of professionalism, kindness, and respect.

A clear sense of self affords me the understanding of how to support the leaders in my life, ensure my leadership initiatives compliment, and strengthen their initiatives. If you strive to self-actualize, providing a clear path for those that might follow becomes easier. Leading is a big responsibility, and you should be respectful of everyone's time.

Professionalism is becoming elusive in today's work environment, but the importance of being kind, respectful, and dressing well cannot be overstated. Never dress professionally to impress others; dress professionally because you hold the organization you serve, its mission, and the people you represent in the highest esteem. I implore you to try it; the quality of your interactions, confidence, and life outlook will increase exponentially almost immediately.

The Power of a Vision. The Importance of a Tribe by Laura Swift
Quad Cities Investment Group, LLC

"I want to be where I choose, not just where I end up." I don't remember who spoke the words, but I'll never forget the statement.

When I entered Ginny's Grow to be CEO group, I was in a place I had not chosen. Suffering the effects of a spinal cord injury, my life had been a whirlwind of activity with little time or ability to think about why I was doing what I was doing or where I wanted to go. I came to Ginny to figure out how to maneuver my world after the injury. I had no idea of the journey that awaited me.

During one exercise, Ginny asked us to draw a map of our lives and identify moments along the way that had most affected our paths. She spoke about difficult times as "crucible moments" that provide opportunities for us to look at things in a different way. And I began to re-frame my life, understanding my "crucible moments" as a gift—opportunities to learn and to grow.

As we shared our stories aloud, the narrative I had created about myself began to shift. The words, weak, worthless, and failure, stood little chance in the face of words like strength, courage, and leader, which were mirrored back to me by the amazing women that surrounded me.

We continued our life-maps by thinking about what we wanted our futures to look like. To be clear, I had no intention of ever becoming CEO of anything. But as Ginny asked questions and allowed space to sit in silence and ponder the answers, I began to understand what it is that I truly care about in life. I began to believe that my life could have a positive impact on others.

And it was sometime during this exercise that the words were spoken: "I want to be where I choose, not just where I end up." The statement resonated with me so deeply that it eventually became my vision, my purpose—the "why" of what I do every day.

"BECAUSE YOU SHOULD LIVE THE LIFE YOU CHOOSE."

These are the first words you read on my bio on my firm's website. That's right. My firm.

Who would've ever thought?!

Learning to be Quiet by Kim Kidwell
Family Museum

When I think of Ginny Wilson-Peters, many words come to my mind immediately: positive, kind, thoughtful, insightful, and observant. When I first met Ginny, I felt like she knew me better than I knew myself as far as how I existed in my work environment. Her leadership style is not one that dictates or tells you how you should handle situations, but rather leads you to come to those conclusions yourself.

As a new manager at the Family Museum, I was cautious as to how to manage people who were formerly my co-workers, and in some cases, formerly above my pay grade. What I realized, thanks to Ginny, is that managing other people starts with being able to successfully manage myself. Setting goals, keeping emotions under control, clear and concise expectations, and taking personal responsibility for my actions and decisions. It is not how people react to me, but how I react to them.

One of the things that made me most uncomfortable was in our one-on-one sessions when there would be no words being said. I always filled the quiet with what I thought Ginny wanted me to say. I dreaded that silence. However, I can say that one of the most powerful things I learned from Ginny was to be quiet. Not an easy task for an outspoken girl from Boston.

The six-second pause before reacting. Let silence do the heavy lifting. Memorable conversations include breathing space. Insight occurs in the space between words. Ginny Wilson-Peters does not need words to describe the type of person she is. She just is as real as it gets.

Forty Challenges for Charity by **Katie Mohasci Pearson**

Last fall, I decided to do something a little different leading up to my 40th birthday, so I reached out to friends and family soliciting 40 challenges to complete by the big 4-0. As I completed each challenge, I donated $40 to the charity of their choice.

After handwriting 40 notes, I donated to the Cystic Fibrosis Foundation. St. Jude's received my donation after I gave blood four times in just under nine months. I handed out 40 flowers to senior citizens and then made a donation to the Alzheimer's Foundation of America. I completed 40 drives at a driving range in less than 4 minutes and made a donation to Beyond Celiac. I made and delivered 40 May Day baskets and made a donation to the Brain and Behavior Research Foundation. I cared for 40 shelter dogs by walking them and playing with them in the yard and made a donation to Last Hope Animal Rescue.

This continued until I had completed 40 such tasks and donations.

Challenges like the 40-hour fast and 40 pull-ups in 40 days pushed me physically and mentally. Many challenges, such as donating 100 hours to our school district, demanded careful planning. I learned how to better shift priorities in order to extend myself. In giving of my time, energy, and money, I received so much more in return. My heart is full and strangers are now friends. I have bettered myself and the community I serve.

The goodness did not go unnoticed. Several friends and family members chose to match my donations, and a few are considering doing something similar for their milestone birthdays. Each of my two daughters decided to follow suit. In a couple months, my youngest turns ten. Lauren is halfway through 10 challenges and donates $10, of her own money, to each charity.

This year was not without adversity. A few months before turning 40, I experienced neuropathic pain and numbness in my left leg and foot. Following weeks of testing, exactly one month before my birthday, I was diagnosed with Multiple Sclerosis (MS). What could have prevented me from completing all 40 challenges, actually reignited the fire to make it happen? Every single one of us has the power to perpetuate positivity and generosity.

Stop and be Mindful by Heather Pederson
American Red Cross

When I first started working for Ginny, we were so busy that our time together was limited. I was newer in my career journey and wasn't experienced in condensing my thoughts and action-items. As a natural extrovert, I got my energy from my interactions with Ginny. With an extremely busy schedule, it was important that our time together was meaningful, but I was a pressurized can of ideas, energy, and social chattiness.

After a couple of not-so-productive interactions, Ginny

made me a mini stop sign that sat on her desk. Out of an ink-jet printed paper stop sign and pencil; yes, she's that creative. Before I would come bounding over, she would hold up the stop sign, which was my indicator to stop and be mindful of the topics and concepts I wanted to discuss. Forcing the hamster, in the wheel, writing post-it-notes in my head to slow down and take a breath (hope you'all enjoy that image and can relate to my lil' buddy the post-it-note writing hamster). To this very day, I've kept this lesson close to my heart. There are so many other nuggets of wisdom that guide my compass. Thank you, Ginny, for being due-north for so many!

Leadership is an Honor by Greg Aguilar
Quad Cities Chamber

To lead others is an honor that is earned but also requires constant maintenance. Most of us think maintenance as something we do to possessions that we own, like a home, a car, or an instrument. Leadership skills, in fact, are personal possessions that depend on the leader to maintain them as well as advance their effectiveness to inspire action and influence others. Leadership is more than being the person in charge of advancing a plan. Leadership is about a personal connection with others and knowing what is in their hearts. Leadership is about building trust and collaborating with those who offer unique talents that will move ideas and actions forward toward success.

I believe that every human being has the ability to lead and influence others, but they must first believe that they are worthy of this honor which inspires others to act. This is a powerful tool that must be respected, for if these skills are used to harm others instead of help, our society will begin to lose its confidence in the leaders of our world. As soon as a leader realizes that they should use their ears twice as much as they do their mouths, the leader's mind will begin to understand what is needed and plans will develop to advance a cause.

The path of a leader is often lonely and there will often be doubt. When doubt emerges, a leader must dig deep into their soul and remember that without their light of leadership, many will be left in the dark.

Believe that you can become a great leader.

Listen twice as much as you talk; this is why we have two ears and one mouth.

Respect the opportunity to lead.

Do the best that you can.

Not a Straight Line to a Destination by Gina Skinner-Thebo
Tone's Spices/B&G Foods

"Losing someone you love is something nearly every single person on earth will experience at some point in their life. And yet, very little can prepare you for the overwhelming sense of loss."

When my best friend from college passed away, I was consumed with grief. I experienced shock, disbelief, and terrible heartache. And then the guilt came.

Living with Rachel's passing has given me a new perspective. It's taught me about grace. It's taught me how to love others more fiercely. It's granted me a new lease on loving people with my whole heart.

The Atwood Center for Women is my way of turning grief and adversity into a living, breathing success story. I'm honoring my friend by talking about the hard stuff. I'm doing my best to give women permission to say to the world, "This is hard. I don't have it figured out. I need help." I'm creating safe spaces for women to come and be brave together.

Leadership comes in many forms. Sometimes you're given a platform and you step up to it. Other times, there's no clear role, but you figure out how to influence those around you.

I don't have it figured out. Every day, I rise with the intention to do as much good as I can, and if I climb into bed at the end of that day knowing I loved well, offered grace, and sat in humility, then it was a good day. If I didn't do any one of those things, I try again the next day.

The mark of a good leader is not never messing up. It's being willing to admit it when you do and then to do everything in your power to make it right. My leadership journey will never be a straight line to a destination. I'm figuring things out along the way and I'm asking others to join me.

Leaders are Not Made by Their Positions by Dougal Nelson
Junior Achievement of the Heartland

Leadership is not a trait or a behavior, nor is it a title. They are not made leaders by their positions. Great leaders are identified by their influence. Their style of communication, the ability to create thoughtful and insightful idea creation, and the careful understanding of personal behaviors of others are fundamental to growing those around them.

Leaders have the uncanny ability to make others want to follow the vision they establish. Communication is a key element in leadership success. Through the vehicle of assenting communication, leaders use positive messaging to encourage others and inspire action. Inspirational motivation should always be at the forefront as they lead both our internal and external stakeholders. Persuasive leaders offer clear and persistent communication to advance change.

They must also stretch others to think more deeply, challenge assumptions, and be innovators. Intellectual stimulation of others is an essential element in helping achieve successful results. They accomplish this through open-ended questions, positive reinforcement, and showing trust in people's strengths and competency.

Leaders must always be focused on the individual. Teams are comprised of many unique attributes. While they must remain focused on the common good of an organization, it is important they are aware that behaviors can differ greatly from one person to the next. Great leaders take the time to show care and concern for individuals. Individualized concern can offer a path to identifying where to place a team member within the organization. Genuine leaders will stand in the shoes of another person to recognize and affirm the strengths of others. They can ascertain opportunities for people to work in their area of expertise.

There is no magic or secret recipe in the ability to lead others. Communicating expectations clearly, inviting and stimulating idea creation, and being responsive to an individual's needs are significant traits leaders employ in their achievement of success.

Twenty Ways to be a Good Leader by **Dave Green Vitalant**

1.   Avoid attempting to do the same things, only harder, that got you promoted in the first place when in a new position.

2.   Be mindful of the unique combination of experience, education, and talent you bring to the table when forming expectations of less experienced employees.

3.   Assume your plans won't work as expected. You'll rarely be surprised, but will be better positioned to intervene.

4.   Don't underestimate the time and energy necessary to sustain change.

5.   Have conversations that matter with your people. People talk about what's on their minds, and what's on their minds is what gets done.

6.   Focus on people instead of numbers when trying to improve the numbers.

7.   Take care of people, but don't coddle them; confidence comes from hard work.

8.   Demand high standards—all else will follow.

9.   Remember your most important, yet most overlooked, role is to develop your people.

10.   Remember if you think everything is going well, you're wrong. Success inspires satisfaction, which in turn, breeds complacency.

11.   Adopt a healthy sense of cynicism about the present and hold an unwavering optimism about the future.

12.   Examine your failures carefully to grow, but avoid long growing seasons. You rarely learn from success.

13.   Be candid with people—on both the good and the bad. We rarely reward strong performers enough, nor do we tend to have direct, yet productive, conversations with people that aren't a good fit.

14.   Remember the vast majority of people want to do a good job. Assuming otherwise will have you catering to the minority.

15.   Seek out responsibility and accountability and expect the same of others.

16.   Master the present and imagine what could be; balancing your time spent on each is critical to achieving your vision.

17.   Don't focus on your competition; it gives them the edge. Be aware but lead the way and let them focus on you.

18.   Understand why your organization exists.

19.   Remember if it feels wrong, it most likely is.

20.   Set the tone for your employees' workplace with positive emotions.

My Ginny Moment by Corey Morrison
On With Life, Inc.

Each of us has those times in our life when we remember clearly as changing the course of our future life. There are the obvious ones, like selecting a college, starting a new job, or moving to a new city. But then there are those life events that more subtly influence us. They are the ones that you might not even realize, at the time they occur, of their course-changing impact. But over the following days, months, and years, you realize something has changed, and for the lucky ones, it has the ability to positively affect not only our own lives but the lives of those around us.

For me, I experienced one of those subtle life influences in 2010 during a University of Iowa MBA Leadership and Personal Development class taught by Ginny Wilson-Peters. I had heard good things about the class from my peers and fully expected going into the class that I would enjoy my learning experience. But what I got out of it was more than just an ability to sit through a class without wishing to be somewhere, really anywhere, else.

Over the course of the six-week intersession class, I was led down a road that forced me not only to challenge my own thinking but to understand my ability to influence others in a positive way. I committed to change, acknowledged my weaknesses, celebrated my strengths, and most of all, I vowed that my leadership journey would never end. It was a life-changing experience for me and one that I hope every leader has the ability to experience. Oprah might call it my AHA moment, I simply call it my Ginny moment.

Leadership Can Start at a Young Age by Angie DeJong
American Equity Investment Life Insurance Company

As a child, I watched my mother get up and go to work every day. She missed many opportunities during my childhood due to work. There was never a doubt in my mind she was a very determined, successful woman. My father was also a hard worker and had many different jobs during my childhood. Seeing my mother so determined, I knew that is how I wanted to be growing up.

The first opportunity I had to work I did. At the age of eight, I had a great-grandmother who didn't get around well and needed her home cleaned and other miscellaneous things done around the house. I drew up a contract for her to sign. I can still remember hearing her laughing at me; she thought this was very professional for an eight-year-old! Regardless of how ridiculous this seemed to her, she signed with a smile. I worked for her every Saturday morning. At her age, the only means of communication besides friends stopping over was the phone. She was ALWAYS on the phone talking about the happenings around town with her cronies, as I called them. Well, it didn't take long for the word to spread to the older women of the community that there was a great, responsible young lady who would love to clean your home, so before I knew it, I had a weekend job cleaning other people's homes as well. I continued this until most of my clients aged past the point of remaining in their homes.

Next, the big summer came at the age of 14. I was finally able to go to work with my mother during the summers. The work seemed very meaningless, most of the summer spent preparing documents for scanning-

removing staples, taping things to paper, but to me, it was a paycheck for the summer. I got to meet new people, understand what leadership was, and understand what having a boss meant as well as real responsibility.

I worked every summer until I was 18. I had a choice of going to college or work. I saw how successful my mother had been without a college education, so I chose to go to work. I didn't want my job to be "because my mom" worked there, so I applied in a different area within the company. I immediately was offered an entry-level position. The position I had accepted had five different levels, so I knew there was an opportunity for growth, so this gave me a goal to strive for. Within nine months, I had hit the level five. Now what?

I had formed a great relationship with a co-worker who was applying for a new position at another company, and she convinced me to do the same. She was hired for the first position she applied for. I had to apply for a couple but finally got in the door in agency services. I had gone from work comp claims to an annuity company. WHAT WAS I DOING??

I quickly learned how to contract and appoint insurance agents. Our department had four individuals who had different functions; I was very curious about learning the other functions. Over the next year, I did learn all the functions and how they interact with other areas of the company as well. I then looked at how some things within the area could be done differently to gain efficiencies. Over the next few years, the department continued to grow. My manager at the time recognized my vision to make the systems and processes operate more efficiently and promoted me to project manager. In this position, I was able to lead the changes within the area to make the necessary improvements. I did this for a couple of years, and as our department continued to grow, they needed a director. My manager moved me into this position. I directed the agency services area for six years.

After mastering that role, my brain needed a challenge. I had formed a great mentorship role with the Chief Operating Officer at the time. The company had an open position for an AML director. This was something new to me and seemed interesting. I talked with him about it, and he had a better idea. He said, "You know, what we need around here is someone who knows how all the systems work across the company. Right now, everyone knows their area and that seems to be it." Our quality assurance area had an opening at that time, so he challenged me to go work in that area for a while and learn the ins and outs of the systems and how the different departments use them. Well, this did sound like a great opportunity to utilize a bunch of my key skills as well as continue to grow my company knowledge.

So I applied for the quality assurance position and was given the opportunity to learn. I learned how annuities went from start to finish through the company as well as many other things. I was able to recommend different solutions to various areas to streamline their processes.

After about two years learning in this area, a new area was formed in our company by our new Chief Operating Officer. It was called the Business Resource Center. This was a vision that he had, a department that sits between the business and the IT department to help bridge the gap across the areas. With the little technical experience from the QA area, and now with the business knowledge I had acquired, I felt this was perfect for me. I applied for and was granted the director role for this area. We worked to build the department from the ground up. I directed the area for about two years before I was promoted to

Assistant Vice President of the area. We had grown from two to eight employees; another year after that, we had another growth spurt and grew to 15, and I was moved to Vice President and now had three directors reporting to me.

As of current, I have been with the company for 20 years and we have grown our staff to include four directors and 16 employees. Our area includes business analysis, project management, and business system security functions.

I have been very fortunate that my mentors were able to see the drive and determination that I have, and that is the first thing I look for in future leaders. I have also been fortunate enough to be able to provide the same opportunities to many other current and future leaders.

I think one of the most rewarding feelings is to see people succeed!

A Journey of the Heart and Mind by Amy Jones
Royal Neighbors

Ten years ago I was starting to feel lost. I was beginning to acknowledge that while work was an important part of my personal satisfaction, I needed more. I was also beginning to question my leadership ideologies and skills. Predictably, I was in my mid-to-late 20s.

I didn't know what to do with these thoughts or even how to articulate them all. I just knew there was something I needed to explore, and I knew that my career path was related to whatever these thoughts would reveal.

While I didn't have the answers, life had already taught

me two things: I find a sense of comfort and control when I engage in learning through books and conversation, and being myself was important to my health and livelihood as I am incapable of faking anything for longer than a few minutes. I hadn't learned what to do with any of this, but I leaned into these unknowns and called Ginny Wilson-Peters.

During her course, I learned that I am on a never-ending journey and that I am not alone. There were women in my group—all that I admire and follow today—who were experiencing similar situations at varying levels. Everyone is on a journey, and everyone is always learning.

My understanding and commitment to leadership have evolved. My definition of leadership changed; I no longer view it as simply a progression to the top, but as a journey of the heart and mind. Ginny provided the space, the connection, and the tools to fuel this journey, and her impact ripples throughout our community. She understands that the greatest leadership reward is paying it forward. Congratulations, Ginny!

Lesson One in Servant Leadership by **Amber Wood OSF Healthcare**

"They" requested leadership lessons/stories from leaders who have impacted Ginny, Integrity Integrated, and the community at large. I thought, *From who? Me?* Wow…what an honor…which leads into part of the next story, lesson, tidbit…

Servant leadership is not full of authority and glamor…it is often filled with leading from behind, bringing light to another's day, cheering from the sidelines, offering encouragement, and even sacrificing of yourself…all in the name of making the world a better place.

My career has been filled with so very many opportunities to be a servant leader through my work with non-profit organizations—but when I pause to look back over life, there were others times in life that I practiced servant leadership…long before I even actually realized I was a leader…

As a child, I knew no stranger…I never had a difficulty starting a conversation with people. And I was always trying to bring comfort to others who were in pain or in need.

Rewind to the early 1980s, the setting was a rural community, population of 600, in northern Illinois, when kids played outside all day and neighbors would keep track of the neighborhood kids—and would even gladly stand in as "grandparents" when needed.

"Grandma Pearl," the neighbor who lived in the next house to the north of my family, wasn't a relative by blood, but she was very much an important person in my life and played an important role through the time she could no longer care for herself and later passed away. Grandma Pearl lived next door for years and loved to sit on the porch and watch the neighborhood comings and goings.

My favorite mode of transportation around the neighborhood was a rusty old tricycle with no tire on the front rim. It served my mom well…she could hear me no matter where I was in the neighborhood, and I clearly knew my boundaries…from our sidewalk to the corner in one direction and from our sidewalk to Grandma Pearl's.

I quickly learned that she also loved tea parties—and tolerated the constant chatter of me as a young child. I was the youngest of three children at the time—and sometimes I was looking for people to pay attention to just me...and Grandma Pearl happily obliged. More importantly, I loved to spend time with her—it was an opportunity to bring sunshine to a woman who was otherwise alone.

If my mom didn't hear my tricycle rim grinding on the sidewalk of the neighborhood, the first place she'd look was at Grandma Pearl's front door. And other times, I would check if Grandma Pearl was sitting on her front porch. If she was, I would holler at her and let her know I would be back shortly. I would invite myself in for a "tea party."

Headed home with a mission..."Mom, I need to take a tea party to Grandma Pearl's house. She's on the front porch. And, Mom, remember she can't have sweets. I'll have a cookie and Kool-Aid...please pack some carrots and water for Grandma Pearl."

No matter what my mom was doing, she'd pause to help me pack up the mobile tea party and deliver the afternoon treats and me, the excited chattering child, back to Grandma Pearl's.

Who would have known that this experience would have such an impact on my life? Learning lessons on how to treat others. One of the greatest lessons I later realized that I had learned through this time spent with Grandma Pearl was that leadership is about building relationships.

At the time, I was just spending time with a neighbor who could offer her full attention to my endless chatter...looking back, it was much more than that. I loved how it felt to spend time with her, building a relationship, and making the world a little brighter for her.

This was one of the first lessons I learned in servant leadership...one that has relived itself time after time in my roles.

Strong Women Tend to Influence and Shape Other Strong Women by **Amanda Hess** **Mississippi Valley Regional Blood Center**

I've respected and admired Ginny as a leader and influencer for nearly 15 years. The first time I saw Ginny present was at a Young Professionals event in Davenport. I believe it was a lunch and learn meeting hosted by the NeXt YP group of DavenportOne. Ginny's story about how she made a major life change from being a president of a printing company to starting her own company as a consultant entrepreneur was fascinating and inspiring to me. She was already accomplished at the top of her game as a young female president in an industry dominated by older males. But the fact that she made a huge decision to leave all that behind to pursue her own dream was incredible to me.

I've heard her story many times since then, but the first time was a pivotal moment in my life. I was just starting to explore my options for career growth as a young female professional. After completing my undergraduate degree and entering the workforce, I knew I wanted a career that provided personal satisfaction along with financial independence. I wanted to do something that mattered to others and mattered to me. Her story validated that I could be successful as a professional doing something I enjoy while helping others. This approach fortified my intent to work in the not-for-profit sector. Her confidence and willingness to take risks has been influential as I have made decisions throughout my career. I see Ginny as a mentor, and I am glad that young women have role models like

Ginny. Strong women tend to influence and shape other strong women. Over the years, I have seen diversity embraced to a greater degree in our community. It is leaders like Ginny that pave the way for others.

Learn Through Doing Your Own Work by Alex Merrin
Self-Employed Coach

I began earning a living as a Transformation Coach in September of 1989, a time when the idea of hiring a "coach" was barely peeking over the horizon. And, the opportunity to pursue this career literally came to me. Prior to this pursuit, I had thirty-six different jobs in twenty years' time. So I can honestly say I experienced thirty-six jobs I didn't want to do.

I had a job as Assistant Promotions Director for a television network and was paid the most money I'd ever made. Yet I was profoundly unhappy and felt trapped by thoughts that only an idiot would give up such high-profile work.

Then it happened. Coming back to the studio one dark and dreary, rainy evening, I took a left turn and plowed into the driver's side of a car coming from the opposite direction. My car was totaled, but I walked away with only a stiff neck. However, the woman in the front passenger seat was pregnant. It was a miraculous blessing that they were uninjured. But I was shaken to the core and knew I needed to remodel my life.

In the first six months of transpersonal training, supported by "learn through doing your own work," I made dramatic changes and began experiencing new outcomes. At some point, I realized if I could make such radical changes in such a short amount of time, anyone could! There was hope for the future and a knowing I wanted to bring this work into the world.

This year, I'm celebrating 30 years of self-support through my coaching practice and the evolving personal changes that have taken me beyond recognition as I've taken leadership of my life.

I'm grateful for every individual with whom I've worked for informing that leadership. I've not once dreaded going to work; actually work has disappeared, leaving only the satisfaction of purpose. Being able to say I get paid for this service I love is a bonus.

Having supported individuals from 16 to 78 years of age from all walks of life, I can honestly say we are just one human family. We all want the same basic things and suffer from similar flavors of the same issues. Yet, we are each a unique expression of this thing called human, like the individuality of the trees that create a forest.

I've seen the myriad of ways we normalize repetitive patterns of thinking and behaving to our own detriment, how blind we are to our lovability, and that the value of a leader lies in their ability to deeply listen from the still point of the heart and how to say the same thing a thousand different ways as if it was the first time.

A NOTE FROM GINNY'S GREATEST SUPPORTER, GREG PETERS

Twenty years ago, the humble beginnings of Integrity Integrated began as Sunday afternoon gatherings out of the living room of our home in Bettendorf. I must state MUCH has changed since the early days. The gatherings have moved to new venues (far and wide). The small gatherings have evolved into a large community of associates and friends. Back then, I was not sure where all of this was going, but look how far your vision and passion has taken you! There are certain milestones in a person's life worthy of pause and reflection; this is indeed one of them.

Twenty years ago, you took a bold leap to change your life path in order to follow a dream. You wanted to help others find their own path toward personal growth and happiness. You led by example, and I firmly believe you have succeeded in making this dream become reality. Look back and cherish what you have been able to accomplish, the lives you have touched.

There is no question in my mind, you embrace each day ready and eager to make a difference. You shine when you have an opportunity to reveal a story about a person who took their own bold leap (with a little nudging).

I'm extremely proud of what you have accomplished and where this journey has taken you. I am anxious to see what the next chapter(s) brings!

With all of my love and endearing support….

Ginny and Greg.

A NOTE FROM THE EDITOR, JODIE TOOHEY

When Shari and Amy approached me to help them put this book together, I was thrilled, mostly because after about six years, I thought maybe my "Get that Wordsy Woman" slogan was finally catching on. I had met Shari and Amy through Ginny when I was attending an event where Ginny spoke. I got to know them a little better through Facebook, by volunteering to lead a workshop at the PR Half-Day Workshop one year, and at the Integrity Integrated Vino Van Gogh event (I still have my painting and have started the practice of creating a new one with my word-of-the-year on my own each year since). I met Ginny when I walked into the management class of the University of Iowa Professional MBA program. At the time, I had been fledgling in my own business for two years, intimidated and my confidence in the toilet. I enrolled in the program because getting a master's degree was on my bucket list, and I thought the knowledge I would gain would help me in my business ventures.

I did learn a lot in my MBA program, and I believe it's helping me, but by far the best classes were the management and leadership classes Ginny taught. Truth be told, comparing costs to benefits, I perhaps could have saved a boatload of money by just taking Integrity Integrated courses. But such is life, and loving school and learning, I'm glad I have the master's degree. Ginny's classes helped me on the road toward clarity of my passion and purpose, and it gave me the confidence to persist in trying to build a livable income through my own business(es).

I'd always loved to write, but through the assessments and reflection Ginny led in her classes, I realized that at least one of the purposes to my writing was helping people say what they want to say, whether that is editing their story, helping them publish it, writing marketing copy, or even simply giving words to something they felt or experienced but couldn't articulate through my own stories.

I wish I could say that's all it took, and I went on to build an immensely successful business. But as Ginny teaches, leadership is a journey. Though I do report more profit on my income tax forms each year, it has been slow going, and I still don't earn a livable income (luckily, my husband has made enough for our family). You see, I've realized that there are many, many ways to help people say what they want to say through writing. At the time of this writing, I essentially have five jobs: owner/operator of Wordsy Woman Author Services, author of eight books (should be nine by the end of 2019), owner/operator of 918studio press, owner/operator of the brand new Legacy Book Press, and volunteer for the Midwest Writing Center, including serving on its board of directors.

I can't tell you how much I've enjoyed working on this book and bringing these words to these pages. I deeply appreciate Shari, Amy, and Ginny for trusting me with this project. I hope I've done them all justice along with everyone who generously contributed their stories, thoughts, and advice. Thank you!

www.ingramcontent.com/pod-product-compliance
Lightning Source LLC
Chambersburg PA
CBHW031900200326
41597CB00012B/502